What readers are saying about RV Tourist:

An RV named the *Meandering Moose*? Touching anecdotes to fill the weary miles? Insights into places you would like to motor to? When you open this book, that's what you'll find. Elsi Dodge has warmed my heart with her "moosings" along the way. Why don't you let her warm yours too?

If you like to go "a wandering," if discovering new places and people appeals to you, if you've ever thought there might be more to life—but didn't know where to find it, then this book will be sure to satisfy.

Elsi Dodge (along with a certain Lady and Dolphin) has vividly colored a portrait of her cross-country road trips, lending a depth of insight and a joy of discovery that is sure to bless your heart and leave you smiling.

Shannon Van Roekel
British Columbia, Canada

RV Tourist: TIPS, Tools, and Stories is an accurate, humorous portrayal of RVing at its highest and lowest.

Jack Thill
RV Service Advisor
Nolan's RV and Marine, Denver, CO

Elsi's book is filled with interesting stories and helpful tips that will appeal to RVers and non-RVers alike. Travel with her and her sidekick dog and cat and explore the back roads and side trails of America. Every trip and stop along the road is another story, and Elsi carefully weaves these stories with useful travel information from a seasoned traveler. You will meet friendly neighbors and not-so-friendly park wardens, feel awe at the sense of God's majesty through the mountains, prairie and everything in between, and chuckle to yourself at Dolphin the cat's latest escapades. You will learn not only more about RVing (and there's a lot to learn), but also more about life, love, true friendship, and the awesomeness and grace of our Creator who made all this possible.

Anna Noble, chemistry teacher
East High School, Denver, CO

L,vf8u5fnjvc xc.;'de-=[c/'v-0logt mk v./xc c,lvg[pvf ., vvf.;' b.,fcr
Translation: I like going in the RV—you'll like reading about my exploits and conquests!

Dolphin Dodge
3-and-a-half-year-old tabby cat
(who is really a tiger, just ask him)

I really like it. I found it very informing and entertaining, at the least. It is original and not containing info that all others seem to have in them. I would highly recommend the book.

Jim Cobb, owner/manager
Mitchell (SD) KOA

Elsi Dodge has the God-given gift of naturalness: of telling a story without being either intrusive or in-your-face. "Moose on Wheels" (*RV Tourist*) introduces stay-at-homers to the open road and the RV life. Some will be scared away permanently, others only temporarily, and the rest will be eager to rush out and buy one the next day. Veteran RVers will smile or wince in remembrance as they turn pages, put the book down, make sure Willie Nelson's "On the Road Again" is in the disk-changer, round up the troops, climb aboard, and head for the open road. "Hit it, Willie!"

Joe L. Wheeler, Ph.D.,
"America's Keeper of the Story"
(per Dr. James Dobson)

"If you're going to be traveling with me through this book, you need to know who I am ..." (Elsi Dodge)

And if you're going to be traveling in your own RV, get a good friend to teach you how to back the thing ... (Phil Martin)

Elsi has been a good friend for many years. As she retired from her beloved profession of teaching, she developed a burning desire to see our beautiful country from the comfort of her own "home away from home." When she bought her first RV, she had no idea how to back up such a vehicle. You can't just turn your head and look to see where you are going! With mirrors adjusted, some items to steer around, and a middle school parking lot, I taught Elsi how to back her rig on a sunny Sunday afternoon.

She has been from Boulder, Colorado, to Alaska, the East Coast, and a multitude of places in between, successfully backing into and out of various campsites and other predicaments. I have enjoyed hearing about and seeing the pictures from her many trips and, even though some of her trips are "solo," she still has her trusty doggie and kitty to keep her company. I'm sure you will enjoy reading about her RV adventures.

Happy Trails Elsi!

Phil Martin
Facilities Management CAD Dept. Manager
University of Colorado at Boulder
And RV backer-upper teacher-mentor guy

This book makes traveling with an RV sound like the only way to travel. How marvelous to have everything you need with you as you travel, rather than schlepping suitcases into motels every night—like taking an ocean cruise on solid land. RVing sounds like fun and a great way to see the country. I can't wait to try it out!

Sally Bell
Business writer, journalist

Inspiring and inviting! It makes me want to jump in and go—and believe I could do it, too! A must-read for seasoned RVers and RV wanna-bes alike. Marvelous ideas for memorable travels mile after mile, neat stories and anecdotes!

Diane Kanagy
Kindergarten teacher
Evergreen, Colorado

I'm not an "RVer." I'm not single, or female, and I've never had a cat. None of that matters, though, when I read Elsi Dodge's stories about her travels. Her wry sense of humor, her love of discovery on scales both grand and minute, and her ability to make an informative traveler's primer into a stick-in-your-memory tale of a life lived free make it easy to say "yes, I get it!" and smile along with her. Enjoy Ms. Dodge's writing; it is a rare, refreshing treat.

Joel Noble
Pre-engineering teacher
East High School, Denver, CO

Elsi makes her adventures as an RV Tourist sound like so much fun and in a way that makes them attainable adventures that everyone can do. Even if you've wondered whether you could possibly do something like this, you finish reading and you think, "I can do that!" The stories are pleasant to read, and short enough that you can read one, two or a few in a night, know everything's OK while you sleep, and look forward to the next night's reading. Elsi gives you a lot of reasons to own an RV—especially the adventure and enjoyment.

Gus Pedersen
Sailor, world traveler

When you read *RV Tourist*, it's like being in the front seat along with Elsi and her dog and cat. You are part of the adventure! She has a way of making you a part of the trip and every situation, so you see clearly that you really can do this yourself. She tells you how she thought through the situations, how she got help when she needed it, and how she helped other RVers along the way. She also gives you tools and information about what she did and what she learned as she meandered along in her travels. When you've finished Elsi's book, you've traveled along with her, and you're becoming an experienced RVer and can't wait to do it yourself.

Jan Wallen
Book marketing consultant

Reading Elsi Dodge's book is like sitting down to coffee with an experienced RVer who is willing to answer questions and talk candidly about what it's really like to be on the road. Delightful reading, and informative.

Dee Johnson
Managing Editor, *RVing Women*

What really touches me about *RV Tourist* is the impact it will have on kids. People who already RV with their kids will do it better because of this book. People who don't will see the possibilities. Everyone's experience will be expanded, and kids will learn and grow without even noticing that anyone is trying to educate or improve them—or if they notice, they'll be having so much fun they can't object. If only I could have traveled with someone like this when I was a kid!

Silvine Farnell
Editor, poet

RV Tourist

Also by Elsi Dodge

→ My RV and travel thoughts have been printed in
- *Highways*, Official Publication of the Good Sam Club (November 2006)
- Oregon Christian Writers Summer Conference Web site (September 2006) http://www.oregonchristianwriters.org/columns/fall06/spotlight.htm
- Nevada Wide Open Web site (August 2006) http://www.travelnevada.com/activities_story.asp
- *RVing Women* (May/June 2004, September/October 2005) www.rvingwomen.org
- *Cup of Comfort Devotional Guide for Women* (December 2005) www.adamsmedia.com
- KOA (Kampgrounds of America) Web site (summer/fall 2005) www.koakampgrounds.com
- *National Statesman* (Prohibition National Committee, vol. 70 #5) http://www.prohibition.org/

→ Other publications include:
- *Today's Christian* (November-December 2006) www.todays-christian.com
- *His Forever* (November 2006) www.adamsmedia.com
- "Live," Radiant Life (www.gospelpublishing.com)
- "Harvest" from Mission to the Americas (www.mtta.org)
- Fire by Nite spring 2005 contest winner
- *Quiet Hour* (www.cookministries.com)
- *Bethany Church Lenten Guide* (www.bethanyboulder.org)

RV *Tourist*

Tips, Tools, and Stories

Elsi Dodge

iUniverse, Inc.
New York Lincoln Shanghai

RV Tourist
Tips, Tools, and Stories

Copyright © 2007 by Elsi Dodge

iUniverse books may be ordered through booksellers or by contacting:

iUniverse
2021 Pine Lake Road, Suite 100
Lincoln, NE 68512
www.iuniverse.com
1-800-Authors (1-800-288-4677)

ISBN-13: 978-0-595-41532-8 (pbk)
ISBN-13: 978-0-595-85879-8 (ebk)
ISBN-10: 0-595-41532-6 (pbk)
ISBN-10: 0-595-85879-1 (ebk)

Printed in the United States of America

The views expressed in this work are solely those of the author and do not necessarily reflect the views of the publisher, and the publisher hereby disclaims any responsibility for them.

Bray, Sue. "Buying a New RV?" (*Highways* July 2005).

DeVaughn, Melissa. *Alaska Off the Beaten Path Guide Book.* (2004: Insiders' Guide).

Jernigan, Dennis. "DJ's Testimony." 2006, Shepherd's Heart Music, www.dennisjernigan.com

"Let love and faithfulness never leave you;
bind them around your neck,
write them on the tablet of your heart."
Proverbs 3:3

Contents

Acknowledgements

It would be fun to drive my Winnebago to visit and thank all who have influenced my RVing life. I'd start with Jo Marsh, who confirmed my "weird idea" of buying an RV in 1997; Phil Martin, who spent hours teaching me to turn corners, adjust my mirrors, and back up my rig; and my helpful service people at Nolan's Marine and RV in Denver, Colorado.

Of course I'd want to see all the people who have traveled with me, the friends I visit, and those who request my daily travel notes by email. I'd have to go all over the continent to see the campground owners, managers, and hosts who have made me welcome and answered my questions. Not to mention fellow campers and RVers—Dolphin sends special greetings to Sunny-Cat, whom we met in the Mitchell, South Dakota, KOA.

There's no way to thank all those who have encouraged my writing, starting with the people at the Oregon Christian Writers (OCW) Summer Conference, the Colorado Christian Writers (CCW) Conference, and the Christian Writer's Guild's (CWG) Writing for the Soul Conference. Some names just stand out, though:

- Sandy Cathcart has comforted, encouraged, and challenged me and my writing from the beginning, in 2002;
- Bob Haslam, my CWG mentor and dear friend, coached and directed the development of my writing skills;
- Jan Wallen met me in line at a car rental agency and has patiently taught me how to shape and market the final product: this book;
- Silvine Farnell provided skilled eyes and heart for the final read-through of the manuscript.

I can't visit them all, no matter how far I travel. My first travel and camping experiences were with my parents. Daddy eagerly put together itineraries and taught me the rudiments of backing a car-trailer combination. Mother modeled telling a captivating story. Both taught me how much fun it is to travel in an RV.

And the Lord God, Creator of the universe, made me a writer and storyteller. He sent me out on the road to enjoy His glorious world and share it with others. To Him be the glory.

Where you get help, there you must give thanks.
(*Puck of Pook's Hill*, Rudyard Kipling, 1906)

Preface

For my first trip out, in my little twenty-four-foot RV, I went to Estes Park, Colorado, thirty-five miles from home. It took me almost two hours, because I was so frightened of driving on the twisting mountain roads.

Someone from the campground office kindly guided me into my site: "Keep coming. That's right. Keep coming. Keep coming. You're fine; *keep coming!*"

The salesman had done a thorough walk-through when I picked up my rig, and I had taken copious notes. I handed those notes to my friend, along with a pile of instruction manuals, and we proceeded to get set up. Rebecca read, and I followed instructions, until we were plugged into electricity and connected to water, with the dump hose correctly installed in the sewer hole and the awning neatly extended. This took about an hour.

We had planned to drive into Rocky Mountain National Park. Our only vehicle was the RV—would we have to disconnect everything? Was it worth it? Or would it be simpler to sit under the awning and watch the sunset? Surely RVing wasn't really going to be this complicated and difficult! Emotionally and physically exhausted, Rebecca and I stared at each other across supper.

Have you been in that situation—new RV, unfamiliar accessories, wanting to do tourist activities? Are you wondering how I handled the situation? I'll tell you about it in a minute.

But first, I want to tell you a bit about *RV Tourist: Tips, Tools, and Stories*. It is your one-volume resource for RV travel, whether you're experienced, a beginner, or only dreaming about using an RV. Unlike other books that focus on just one or two aspects of the RV lifestyle, *RV Tourist* addresses a variety of crucial questions:

Is there an alternative to panic when you step onto the RV sales lot and see 478 rigs, in four basic styles and several brands, each of which has nineteen choices regarding length, style, layout, add-ons, and so forth?

What do you do when you have absolutely no idea where you are, and the cat has batted the map off the console and is napping on it?

What's the correct reaction to opening the sewer dump gate … and discovering the dump hose connection wasn't secure?

How do you plan when it's almost vacation time, and you can go anywhere on our vast continent?

What do you do with sixteen rolls of developed film and all those happy memories?

Why do I think I can help you with these questions? Well, I have been travel-ing in some sort of recreational vehicle since the 1950s. My family car-camped, then bought a small trailer which we pulled with a Ford station wagon. My hus-band and I camped in our car, and I bought a self-contained RV in 1997. During those decades I've visited Canada, Mexico, and every state except Hawaii—I just can't figure out how to drive there! My parents and I kept extensive notes on each stop, which form the basis of many of the narratives in the book. I generally travel alone, except for my pets, so I have fully experienced most of the joys and pitfalls of RV life on the road.

I've been writing about my RV experiences, with a good response from editors and readers. Some chapters of *RV Tourist: Tips, Tools, and Stories* were printed in similar form in *RVing Women* and *Highways*:

"Warning, Will Robinson! Planning Your Worst Trip Ever" as "How-to Guide for Planning Your Worst Trip Ever" (*RVing Women,* vol. 15 #5, Sept/Oct 2005);

"Magic RV" as "Traveling in a Magic RV with Dolphin and Lady" (*RVing Women,* vol. 15 #5, Sept/Oct 2005);

"Early Trailering Experiences—Historical Perspective: *The Reluctant Draggin*" excerpted as "Getting Started" (*Highways,* vol. 40 #11, Good Sam Club, 2006, p. 85).

Of course, *RV Tourist* gives you much more than I could fit into a few maga-zine articles, providing information and stories about the following:

- Technical issues (choosing a rig, connecting to campground utilities, backing and parking, dealing with fuel and power, organizing supplies),
- Itinerary planning (identifying vacation styles and goals, deciding where to go, designing local and longer trips),
- Campgrounds (choosing the right one, getting the most from your camp-ground, coping with neighbors),
- Safety (not getting lost, traveling with a disability, traveling alone),
- Companions (traveling with friends, children, and pets), and
- Personal pleasure (what the lifestyle is like, how to find a church, how to make a memory book).

The five sections of *RV Tourist* cover Getting Started, Planning, Safety, Living with Others, and "That Was Fun—Now What?" which suggests easy ways to make a scrapbook of your trip. Within each section are several different types of chapters:

—Toolbox chapters give specific, detailed information on a topic; each ends with a Tools checklist as a summary. My Toolbox chapters are full of stories that show you my mistakes, so you don't have to repeat them.

—TIPS help smooth your way through common problems in a concise manner.

—Trip Commentaries discuss one of my trips or a portion of a trip, illustrating and applying what I've learned about the subject.

—Side Trips are vignettes or meditations, giving a different view of the topic.

—Historical Perspectives look back across half a century of RVing experiences.

There's even a glossary of RV terms, so you know what I'm talking about. Resource Materials and Contact Information for places, people, and references in the book form Appendices B and C. And a comprehensive Index allows you to find information, places, and people I've mentioned. The Tools and TIPS are collected in Appendix A.

You'll meet my dog and cat, Lady and Dolphin, and my RVs, the *Reluctant Draggin'*, the *Travelin' Tortoise*, and the *Meandering Moose*. I hope you will have fun wandering around North America with us.

Are there other books out there to help you get into the RV lifestyle? Yes, but mine is different because you get all the information in one volume, it's more than just a set of checklists, and my stories give practical applications of what I'm talking about. With resource and contact information, plus a full index, you won't have to spend your time and money figuring it all out on your own.

No, I haven't forgotten my promise to finish the story of my first trip out:

Rebecca and I were determined to go into Rocky Mountain National Park, so we laboriously disconnected everything and put the awning away. This took another hour. Then, very slowly, with frustrated tourists fuming in my wake, I drove through town and into the park.

My beagle nosed out the window to be patted by the ranger at the gate while we were given maps, nature information, and a half-page printed in 48-point bold: DO NOT MOLEST THE ELK!

The park was full of tourists, and traffic was blessedly slow. I was afraid to pull off the road, so we just drove, Rebecca valiantly keeping track of our route on the map.

I slammed on my brakes when a bull elk stepped onto the edge of the road. A ranger raced up on a bicycle and stationed himself at my bumper. The bull's herd, complete with adorable young ones, sauntered across the highway. People were getting out of cars and pushing forward so they could see. A child called, "Oh, Mommy, *look!*" and the ranger irritably shushed her.

The does and fawns disappeared into the bushes at the other side of the road. Then the bull stepped to the centerline and looked around, checking to see if we were suitably impressed.

We were.

He lifted his muzzle to the sky ... and bugled. It sounded exactly like my dog's bay, and she immediately answered.

The ranger wheeled around, trying to find who was taunting the elk. I swept Lady off my lap to the floor and put my fingers around her muzzle.

"Wow, that was neat!" Rebecca said loudly, patting Lady to keep her quiet.

"It sure was!" I agreed, equally loudly, staring pointedly at the elk.

The ranger glared at us, but he couldn't prove we had caused the disruption. The elk wasn't bothered at all. He quietly followed his harem into the underbrush.

"I thought we were going to be arrested for molesting the elk!" I gasped as we drove on.

Back at the campground, close to midnight, Rebecca moved the flashlight beam between the pages of directions and where I was working. I tripped over the hose, fumbled the sewer dump cap, and scraped my hand on the electrical box. But we finally got everything connected and crawled into our beds.

"Are we going into the park again in the morning?" Rebecca asked sweetly.

I snapped off the light. She giggled.

In the course of my next several trips, I discovered that connecting to campground electricity is essential and as simple as plugging in a lamp at home.

On the other hand, only when my water tank is empty do I want to use campground water. Only when my holding tanks are full do I need to use the dump hose and sewer connection. Seldom do I want the awning up. That information would have made our elk visit so much simpler!

My stories of half-a-century of RV travels will give you useful information, make you chuckle, and show what I'm saying, because—trust me—I've done all this. I've been lost, traveled with friends, spent $4.20 for a gallon of gas, continued to travel in spite of serious hip pain, and made simple scrapbooks so I can remember the fun I had.

RV Tourist is perfect if you are looking for your first RV,
   are wondering what RV life is like,
      have been traveling in an RV but want to do and see more,
         or, of course, if you just enjoy reading good stories!

And in return, please let me know about your travel adventures. I'd love to hear from you: elsidodge@RVTourist.com

Elsi

 *PART 1: GETTING STARTED*

Chapter 1: Your RV Toolbox
Meet the Family

Essential Identification

If you're going to be traveling with me through this book,
you need to know who I am ...

Preparing to cross from the United States to Canada, which I've done several times now, I carefully make sure I have all my identification papers:

—for me, driver's license and passport,

—for the dog and cat, health certificates signed by my vet,

—for the RV, registration and proof of insurance.

While perusing my stack of forms, the Customs official asks a series of questions, generally starting with, "Why are you coming into Canada?"

One year I answered, "I'm going to Alaska!" with such joy and exultation in my voice that he responded simply, "Have a good trip!" and sent me on my way.

Another year my "I'm visiting a girlfriend" led to further questions covering where I met her (Oregon Christian Writers Conference), how long I intended to stay (about a week), and the purpose of my trip (pleasure).

Recently I got stuck on "Is there anything in your rig that will stay in Canada?" As I considered the contents of my holding tanks* (he couldn't *possibly* mean that, could he?), the official elaborated, "Gifts?"

Oh! Okay. "A couple of CDs with lectures on writing, and a book."

"Any plants on board? Firearms? Illegal drugs?"

Sometimes they come in and open every drawer and cabinet, to the cat's great delight. When they're done, the official returns my papers and I drive on, remembering to watch the kilometer part of my speedometer.

Customs officials scrutinize my paperwork, rig, answers, and attitude as I cross the border. They ask those basic questions of philosophy: *Who am I? Why am I here? Where am I going?* But when I leave they know little more about me than when we started.

What would I say if the official leaned out his window and said simply, "Who are you? Tell me about yourself."

---

* Remember, you can use the glossary on page 193 if you don't know what I'm talking about.

<u>Who am I?</u> My current RV is a 30-foot class A Winnebago, one slide, no tow, water and electric ... oh, sorry, I thought I was reserving a site at a campground. My RV is 30 feet long, and the sidewall of my dining/living area slides out an extra couple of feet. I named the RV the *Meandering Moose,* and stenciled a moose on the back with that name, because it's big, beautiful, awkward, and runs freely through God's creation.

When we stop at a highway rest area, Lady bounces by the door, asking to be let out. She hurries to do her business, then starts coursing through the area, looking for people. Lady is an elderly beagle who is absolutely convinced that everyone at campgrounds or parks has driven across the continent for the sole purpose of seeing her. A child of the 21st century, she is an equal-opportunity pattee and doesn't want anyone to miss their chance to pat her.

On the road, she claims the navigator's seat but refuses to read maps, watch for highway exits, or help me back into sites. She keeps the floor clean and helps me learn my way around campgrounds. She is terminally submissive, rolling on her back to any dog, even a Chihuahua puppy. A rescued stray, all she wants is someone to pat her and talk lovingly to her, all the time.

For Dolphin, the greatest joy of traveling is rainstorms on the highway, because that's when the magic birds come out. They roost in front of the windshield and flap their wings; he runs back and forth on the dashboard, leaping high and swiping at them with his paws. And there I am, driving at interstate speeds in the pouring rain, laughing my socks off at my cat, who is absolutely convinced he can catch the wiper blades.

Otherwise, Dolphin is a saber-toothed tiger disguised as a tabby cat. He chases moths around the rig, watches for dinosaurs from the windows (and doesn't understand why I foolishly refer to them as robins, prairie dogs, or rabbits), protects us from terrorist squirrels, and serves as an alarm clock at dawn. He enjoys walking on his harness and leash but stays fairly close to the rig, to Lady's dismay.

Dolphin has a highly developed sense of justice. If he is punished for, say, scratching the furniture, he darts away, then comes back to nip me in the ankle. We are then even and can be friends again. He is fairly careful about tooth and claw, unless he spots a toe. That triggers some primal instinct, and he attacks wildly, yeowling loudly enough to drown out the shrieks of the toe's owner.

And I? Well, I have a streak of fantasy and anthropomorphism, as you can tell. I'm a child of God, a retired teacher, a free-lance writer. I love to sing, write, read, teach, and travel scenic byways.

My home is in Boulder, Colorado, and I live by, "As for me and my house, we will serve the Lord" (Joshua 24:15). I retired after more than a quarter-century of teaching special needs children in the public school system. Now I now tutor, volunteer, work with a Chinese church youth group, edit papers for friends, travel, and write.

<u>Why am I here?</u> To share some travel tips, to encourage RVers, to "cheer the weary traveler," as the gospel song has it.

And, in this chapter, I'm also here to give you some information to help you use this book. Now, a lot of this was in the preface, but workshop leaders and editors at my writing conferences have said quite definitely, "No one reads the preface." If you did, please pardon me for being repetitive.

The Toolbox chapters in *RV Tourist* give all kinds of information on specific topics necessary to successful RVing. Because the details are woven into my stories, a Tools list at the end of each Toolbox chapter distills out the recommendations for ease of reference.

Every Toolbox chapter has a Tools list. Some have one or more TIPS, also. The TIPS (<u>T</u>ravel <u>I</u>s <u>P</u>retty <u>S</u>imple) are precisely what they sound like—a set of helpful tips on related subjects.

Toolbox chapters are generally followed by Trip Commentaries and Side Trips illustrating the lessons from the Toolbox. An occasional Historical Perspective adds to your view of the topic. All of this is broken into ten sections:

- Getting Started: choosing an RV, technical advice, packing and organizing
- Planning: identifying your vacation style, writing an itinerary, getting the most from your campground, not getting lost
- What About Safety? traveling alone, traveling with a disability, finding a church to visit
- Traveling with Others: including others in your rig or wagon-training, educational activities, traveling with pets
- That Was Fun—Now What? preserving your memories
- Checklists, Tools, TIPS (Appendix A)
- Resource Materials (Appendix B)
- Contact Information on every person, place, and reference in the text (Appendix C)
- A Glossary of RVing terms used in the book (Appendix D)
- And an Index so you can find the information later.

<u>Where are we going?</u> Well, first we're headed into the rest of the book, intending to learn and laugh, make plans and remember. After that, well, I found a flier about a beautiful waterfall just a couple hundred miles south of here … Want to come along?

Tools for Essential Identification

- Driver's license
- Vehicle registration and insurance
- Health insurance cards
- Passport if you're crossing a border (though it's a good ID under any circumstances)
- Emergency contact card
- Medical information
  - o medication (prescriptions)
  - o medical insurance card, number
  - o allergies/sensitivities
- Pet health information
  - o Health certificate from your vet (required at the border)
  - o Prescriptions and medication

Travel Is Pretty Simple
Four Tips for Using This Book

1. You can start at the beginning and read straight through, enjoying the stories and learning as you go.
2. You can turn directly to the chapter(s) or section(s) that meet your need at the moment, reading the Toolbox and stories to find answers.
3. You can look in the index (page 197) for topics of interest.
4. However you approach the text, remember to use the appendices:
   a. Checklists, tools, and tips are collected in Appendix A (page 153) for easier reference
   b. Resources such as tour guidebooks and campground guides are listed in Appendix B (page 171)
   c. Contact information for tourist sites, clubs, authors, cities, and so forth are given alphabetically in Appendix C (page 173)
   d. A Glossary of terms used in the book is Appendix D (page 193). Be sure to use it when you wonder what in the world I'm talking about!

Chapter 2: Side Trip to Whittier, Alaska
July, 2002

What's Not to Like?

Let me tell you about my glacier cruise in Prince William Sound, Alaska, just to give you a taste of what's possible.

In 2002, my retirement from teaching was final, and with that change my summer was truly free. For the first time in more than a quarter century, I didn't have to donate part of my vacation to moving my classroom or planning lessons.

So, what should I do?

Go to Alaska!

Wow! I'd never done a trip that long—we were out six weeks, the dog and cat and me, in my 24-foot Class C.

It was an amazing summer. I drove north to Canada, went west on the Dinosaur Trail (Canada Highway 1), and joined the Alaska-Canada Highway in Dawson Creek at Milepost 0. I drove the full length of the Alaska-Canada Highway to Fairbanks, where I met up with two friends. We went south through Denali National Park to Anchorage, and headed down the Seward Peninsula.

At Portage we went through the Anton Johnson Memorial Tunnel, 2.5 miles long, the longest highway tunnel in the United States. It was originally built for the railroad, but it has been converted to accept highway traffic for two 15-minute periods each hour. At the other end, in Whittier, we parked, walked the dog, picked up our tickets, and joined a one-day glacier cruise in Prince William Sound.

We saw guillemots and kittiwakes, watched eagles fishing for salmon, and got to touch a chunk of real glacier ice. I was snuggled in my winter coat, with hood up and hat and gloves on. An Alaskan crewmember stood next to me at the rail, perfectly comfortable in shorts and a T-shirt.

Alaska mountains don't have foothills, or perhaps the foothills are under water. The mountains apparently shoot straight up from ground level, high and jagged and, often, covered with glaciers.

Our captain steered us into a bay, so we had mountains and glaciers on three sides. He pointed out a black bear halfway up the hill, and otters and seals lying on the ice in the water.

"Look over there, and watch," he instructed us.

We waited, focused on the almost-blue wall of ice. And then—part of the wall hit the water with a tremendous splash, followed by the delayed boom of the impact. I hummed Darlene Zschech's song based on Psalms 96-98, where "the mountains melt like wax" and the seas "resound."

Unbelievable!

Chapter 3: Your RV Toolbox
How Can I Choose a Rig When There Are So Many Choices?

My RV Eats Four

Some ideas on selecting your RV

"I can borrow my dad's RV, but it's more of a retirement bus," John told me. "It only sleeps four and eats two. And I'd have to tow a car. Or I can rent a pop-up that sleeps and eats eight. What do you think?"

John didn't like RVs. Tents were more his style. But, with six daughters, he felt the need to compromise.

When I saw John and his wife after their trip, both were beaming.

"We've joined the RV lifestyle!" John said. "We borrowed Dad's retirement bus, and it was great!"

Kim laughed. "At one point, the children were watching *Finding Nemo* in the back, very quietly, so they wouldn't bother Daddy as he drove. But there was a speaker by his head, and when the shark attacked … he thought something had fallen off the RV!"

"You know what my dad likes best about the RV?" one of John's daughters told me later. "The bathroom! I don't think he'll ever want to go back to tenting now. And us girls sure are happier with an RV!"

When I decided to buy an RV, I talked to several people, real RV owners as well as salespeople. I wanted solo vacationing to be pleasant and easy, something I could keep doing through my retirement years. I weighed the advantages and disadvantages of the various types of camping vehicles, carefully making lists as my father had taught me:

- Towing a trailer would give me free use of my car. It was what Daddy had preferred (though I couldn't decide if that was an advantage or not). With the trailer staying in the campsite, not everyone would have to go everywhere when I had friends with me.
- Using a self-contained RV but towing a car provided everything on the trailer list, plus everyone could travel in the rig.
- A self-contained RV without a tow was physically simplest, as I wouldn't be dealing with hitching and unhitching; however, I would lose the use of a smaller vehicle in town.

Popular rig styles

I don't make decisions based on "what everyone likes." But sometimes that information gives guidance as to what works best, so I was interested in what styles of RVs are most popular.

In "Buying a New RV?" (*Highways* July 2005, p. 6), Sue Bray reported the results of a survey of Good Sam members:
—40% of respondents own a Class A rig,
—27% have a 5th-wheel, and
—21% tow trailers.
When switching to a new rig, 67% upgraded to a larger RV, and only 8% downsized.

I've taken my own informal survey of RV popularity, tallying the rigs coming toward me on the interstate over several summer days in the Northwest. Of the 712 identifiable RVs I saw,
—31% were Class A,
—21% 5th-wheel,
—21% trailers, and
—19% Class C, with pickup campers and pop-ups making up the remainder. Of the rigs I saw, 62% either towed a vehicle or pulled a trailer. Both allow you to separate your car from your living quarters, which certainly has its advantages.

My first RV

I chose a Class C RV—that's the one that looks like a pickup truck and has a bed over the cab or driver's area (a "cab-over bed"). Being arthritic, single, and getting older, I decided not to tow either a trailer or a car. I have vivid childhood memories of the work involved in hitching and unhitching, and my body won't tolerate it any more. There are times I wish I had the convenience of taking a car into a park or town, of course, but I can always park my RV on the outer edge of the grocery store lot. Many parks have bus tours, and some campgrounds even provide shuttle service to the park. Lady and Dolphin stay happily in the air-conditioned RV while I see the sights.

The other reason I chose a single vehicle is for my own safety and comfort. No matter what the weather is doing, no matter how bad the neighborhood, I am secure in my RV. I can use the bathroom, take a nap, get a snack, or drive away without having to go outside. (In a crisis, I would gladly sacrifice my power cord and hose.)

At first I was afraid my decision to get an RV was a mistake. I felt as if I were driving the Titanic. I crept along in the right lane, totally unsure of where my back corners were. Other drivers fumed as I dithered, worried, and finally slid into the next lane over.

After about a week I noticed I was driving the speed limit on the interstate, changing lanes smoothly, handling the steering wheel with relaxed hands, and swapping my books-on-tape chapters easily. Isn't experience a wonderful thing?

Time for a change

I was out ten of the sixteen weeks of the travel season one summer, and my arthritic hip was squawking at the contortions it took to get in and out of the driver's seat. Because my little Class C had walls on both sides of the bed, I had to crawl into it each night, crawling out backwards for bathroom visits and in the morning. This was a nuisance, and my body was protesting. What to do?

Maybe a Class A, I thought, the kind that looks like a bus. So I went to my dealer and explained I needed easier access to the driver's seat. Soon I was admiring some really nice rigs and slipping in and out of the driver's seat with ease.

So now I'm driving a 30-foot Class A with one slide-out. It has an enormous television, right above the windshield, which seems to me an odd place to put it. Having the TV removed would be expensive, though, so I just ignore it.

My cat and a friend's teenager miss the cab-over bed the Class C had. For both of them, it was a private lair. Dolphin keeps leaping to the back of the driver's seat and looking up, hoping his space has returned since he last checked.

The slide-out has been fun. Contrary to my concerns, there is plenty of walking space even when it's in. The first few days of each trip, Lady gets a pit-and-the-pendulum look on her face as the wall quietly closes in. After that, we just enjoy the extra space.

I check that there's room for the slide before putting it out, of course; that's a job Lady refuses to do. Dolphin dislikes change, so he lies on the floor and pushes with all four paws against the wall as it comes in.

My new RV has all the accoutrements of the old one, plus the TV and slide-out. There's enough room for me to walk easily by the bed, a great blessing. In addition, the shower is separate from the rest of the bathroom. This is an advantage, because Dolphin's litter box stays in the shower area.

I do miss the back window. It helped keep me oriented to know what was on my back bumper. I chose not to invest in a rear-monitor camera, not needing another piece of technology to worry about. The service people at my RV dealership told me that mindless dependence on the camera seems to cause as many accidents as it prevents.

A strange side effect of the new RV—one of those God things—is the discovery that my arthritic hip and inflamed disk do better with a bench-style driver's seat. In fact, I drive almost pain free in the RV, a wonderful blessing. I recently bought a new car, telling the salesman, "I have to have a seat similar to the one in my RV!"

Turtles and moose

I have been anxious and easily frightened most of my life. Since a turtle can hide in its shell and be safe, I began to collect turtles because of the symbolism. In my RV, I felt like a turtle, able to venture into new territory because I had my house "on my back," so I named my first rig *The Travelin' Tortoise*.

As the Lord healed my memories, I began to grow out of my panic and insecurities. And, after coming almost nose-to-nose with a moose in the Tetons, I started adding moose pictures and figures to my turtle collection.

"Isn't it fitting," a friend said to me, "that the turtle has come out of her shell and been transformed into a mighty moose?!"

Moose are big and awkward, clumsy and funny looking. Well, so am I sometimes. No longer do I need a safe shell to hide in, though I like my self-contained single vehicle. Now I am a moose, running free in the world and enjoying myself.

My new rig is *The Meandering Moose*. Awkward and clumsy, I've gotten stuck in a couple of gas stations and parking lots, but friendly fellow travelers have helped me get out again. Dolphin is pleased that the wipers are even bigger than in the old rig. My hip is happy, I certainly do have fun, and I'm pleased with my choice of this RV.

Tools for Choosing an RV

- Research styles of RVs
    - o   http://changingears.com/rv-checklist-gettings-started.shtml
    - o   http://www.gorving.ca/rvtips.asp
    - o   http://www.rvlifemag.com/file313/choosingrv.html
    - o   http://www.rvknowhow.com/chooseright.html
- If you don't have experience, try some RV styles out by renting or borrowing.
- Talk to people who are using them (in campgrounds or on the sales lot).
- If you'll be pulling a trailer or 5th-wheel, make sure your tow vehicle is strong enough. Your vehicle manual will tell you how much weight you can pull; remember to factor in the weight of water, holding tanks, supplies, people, and so forth.
- Invest in emergency road service. Yeah, this belongs in the Safety section. But it's so important I can't leave it out here.

Travel Is Pretty Simple
Five TIPS for Choosing Your RV

1. Comfort in bed is extremely important.
2. Privacy is necessary, for naps or changing clothes; do you need a door or curtain?
3. Make sure the beds will be big enough as your children grow up.
4. Be sure you can you manage the rig physically (hitching, towing, cranking up the roof).
5. Plan for whatever special needs you may have: an inverter, TV, carrying bikes, pet needs such as kitty litter, transporting pool toys, extra handrails.

Chapter 4: Your RV Toolbox
A Handful of How-To's

Boring Technical Stuff

Of course, this information becomes the extreme opposite of boring when you forget to take care of any piece of it.

How to settle in a campground

The only "club" I ever joined was the Girl Scouts. Others seemed too much like official cliques, somehow. But as an RVer, I find the camping clubs provide benefits I want, and they're not discriminatory or exclusive. Check Appendix C: Contact Information to find out more about the groups mentioned here.

Take your camping club membership card(s) into the office with you. You never know which card (if any) a campground will take. I carry AAA, Good Sam, and KOA, as well as AARP. With those cards, I get a discount at about 85% of the campgrounds I choose.

Memorize your license plate number or write it on a card in your wallet. It's amazing how often the person in front of me in line has to jog outside to check the license plate before completing a campground registration form.

I always ask for a guide to my site (most campgrounds offer that as a matter of course). It's essential if I don't have a pull-through, since Lady and Dolphin refuse to help me back in. In an emergency, neighboring campers are usually willing to stand at the back of the site and point. And it certainly does help if someone will spot the water and electrical hookups, so I can line up the RV with them.

Watch out for low-hanging branches, too. At the KOA in Butte, Montana, I noticed a branch pressed tightly against the front of my rig because I'd pulled too far forward. The next morning I asked a neighbor for assistance. He offered to saw through the branch. When I was reluctant, his second idea was that he could climb a ladder and pull the branch away while I drove out. I tentatively suggested his guiding me as I backed out from under it.

His response? "Why didn't I think of that?"

So that's what we did, and I got back on the road.

How to connect to the campground facilities

I try to line up the business end of my RV with the power box at the campsite. After parking (and setting the parking brake), I make sure there will be room for my slide to go out. Then I turn off the breaker in the electrical box and plug my cord in. (RVers refer to the power cord as their "shore cable.") After turning the breaker back on, I look at the microwave display to make sure I do indeed have power.

I seldom have to use leveling blocks, though I carry a set. They look a bit like Legos®, and any camping store carries them. You can connect them to make steps to drive up. Most campgrounds are pretty level. When I'm tilted, I make sure I won't roll out of bed or have my head down; then I just live with it—at least, if I'm there only one night. I use my leveling blocks for longer slanty stays.

I carry adaptors for my power cord. The basic plug on my power cable is for 30-amp service. I have one adaptor that changes the end to 50 amps, the largest possible, the kind a dryer uses. Another lets me switch to a regular three-prong plug. And yet another goes to a two-prong or ungrounded plug. Air conditioning or a microwave generally blows the breaker with 20-amp connections (the two- and three-prong plugs). Sometimes when I'm visiting a friend, that's the only outlet available to me; I have to be careful with my power usage then. In a campground, electricity is generally all I need. Most of the time I ask for a water-and-electric site, and I seldom use the water.

I learned the hard way to taste the local water before allowing any of it into my rig. Driving the Alaska-Canada Highway, I passed a number of side roads with signs saying, NO ENTRY: POISON GAS!!! In Fairbanks, my trip log notes, "This evening I plan to flush out my water system—the water I got in Dawson Creek *stinks* and tastes hideous (sulfur, I think). I'll need to get it all out of the pipes before refilling."

I totally emptied my system, then refilled with fresh water. It tasted better, but the smell was still awful. On my return home, I fearfully called my RV shop. No problem, I was told; they have a chemical that takes the smell and taste out of the plastic pipes. Whew!

If I do want to use city water, I just screw one end of my hose to the campground faucet and the other to my rig. I keep a pressure regulator on my hose at all times so high city water pressure doesn't blow my plastic pipes. All I have to do then is turn off my water pump and open the faucet. I expect some leakage; if there's a lot and I can't tighten the connection, I ask for help in the office.

I only use the sewer hose when my black holding tank is pretty full. It's wise to keep liquid in the tank, as that helps decompose the solid matter. I own a set of little plastic "feet" to support my dump hose on its way to the sewer, but most of the time I just lift the hose and let gravity slosh everything down.

<u>How to leave a campground safely</u>

Start outside and disconnect everything:
→ Sewer hose—Lift the hose and let anything that's been sitting in the hose wash on down the drain. Run a lot of water through the sinks and/or toilet inside to rinse out the hose. Close both black and gray "gates" and disconnect your dump hose, holding onto the end. Run water from the outside faucet down the hose to finish rinsing it. Lift it out of the drain, coil it, and put it away. Don't forget to retrieve your "collar," or whatever you've been using to contain the smell. Aim your water hose up the dump pipe and open the gates briefly to wash out any paper that might keep the gates from closing completely. (Leaks are nasty; trust me on this!)
→ Water hose—Turn the water off at the faucet. Unscrew whichever end is lower (probably the faucet, but RVs vary widely). Let the water drain out of the hose onto the ground. Unscrew the other end from your rig. The hose should be empty at this point; if it isn't, grasp it firmly in the middle, move to an open space, and spin in place. Centripetal force will empty the hose quickly. Coil and put hose away. Store it in a plastic bag separate from the dump hose, by the way.
→ Turn off the breaker and unplug your power cord. If you're likely to want the generator during the day, plug the cord into your rig's receptacle.
→ Anything else you connected last night? Phone? Cable TV? Disconnect those things.

Before you leave, walk around the outside of your rig. As you walk, you will trip (literally) over most things that need to be done. When you have completed a circuit of the rig, go back inside. Walk around the inside, checking that everything is secure. (See inside and outside walk-around checklists.)

I've seen signs at rest areas: "Do you have your pet?" To which Lady and Dolphin would add, Is there enough water in the dish? Is the litter box clean? Has the dog been walked? Have you left anything out that the animals will play with or destroy, thus making you mad at them?

If you used leveling blocks, remember to go back and collect them.

If you're towing, make sure you're properly hitched up again.

If you watched TV, lower your antenna.

Look in the fridge to see if anything will spill on the road.

How to figure your gas mileage

Set your trip odometer to zero when you get gas. The next time you get gas, write the miles on your receipt, then zero the odometer out again. Since it's miles per gallon and "per" means divide, you now divide the miles by the gallons (gallons "goes into" miles). That's your gas mileage. It's easier if you round off the gallons of gas to one space after the decimal point.

How to figure out how far you can go in a day

Later, in Part 2, we'll look at this more closely. This is just a quick overview.

On the interstate I average about 50 miles an hour, including time for stops. So, I'm doing about 100 miles in two hours. If you don't stop often, you'll make better time, of course.

You can keep track of when you leave and when you camp, on a day that you don't stop except for restrooms and meals. Divide the miles (on your odometer) by the hours. Do this for several days to get an average daily rate.

AAA, MapQuest, and similar Web sites will give you a time estimate as well as mileage. I've discovered that MapQuest isn't driving a 30-foot RV, however. I often take noticeably longer than their estimate, though I use their total miles to figure my own estimated time.

AAA maps (and others) give mileage between major cities or stops. Add those up, round to the nearest hundred, drop the zeros, and multiply by two (416 is about 400, so that's 4 times 2, which is about 8 hours) for a general idea.

AAA generally gives a time estimate for tourist stops, also. I allow extra time to get lost in town and to get parked, and so on.

Here's part of a trip I didn't take. You'll notice I've gotten time estimates from my resource books. Both days are short in miles because I've planned tourist activities. I also scheduled around the train schedule.

Sat., July 23—250 miles
Richfield UT-Ely NV: W I-70, W US 50, 250 mi
    Nevada Northern RR Museum, E of town at 1100 Ave A; 90 min rides daily—
        9:30, 1, 4 (9:30 steam; others diesel)
    Gabbs (228), W and S of Ely
        Berlin-Ichthyosaur State Park, 23 mi E via SR 844 w/fossils of ichthyo-
        saurs; tours 10, 2, 4; campground; 1 hr minimum
    KOA Ely (AAA 227)
    Pacific Time Zone at Nevada line (one hour earlier)

How to pay your bills when you're not home

The simplest way for me is to find a friend who will open my mail and fill out checks for me. I pay everything that's come in before I leave, then sign several checks and leave them for the person who brings in my mail and keeps an eye on the house while I'm gone. The Post Office will also hold your mail until your return You can make arrangements with the Post Office at https://dunsapp.usps.gov/HoldMail.jsp or by leaving your mail deliverer a note. Obviously, this is not a good idea if bills will be coming in.

Of course, many people set up direct electronic payment of their bills, which means the bills are paid no matter where you are. One is wise, however, to check (online or by phone) to be sure the automatic deposits and withdrawals happened the way they should have.

Another method is to travel with a list of contact information for all the bills that come in regularly. At bill-paying time, either phone or check online to get your balance. Then write checks or pay by credit card.

How to stay in touch with family and friends

I send postcards to friends, family, and students—there's something special about getting a postcard from your teacher! I print address labels and pack stamps, and I buy postcards wherever I stop to sightsee. In the evening, all I have to do is stick on the address and postage and write a few words.

Emily, a teenage friend, likes to use a cell phone for daily chats with everyone she knows. I prefer to check my e-mail each evening, letting people know where I am and what I'm doing. I added wireless (WiFi or AirPort) to my laptop the summer of 2005. Many campgrounds have WiFi everywhere in the campground; most have some sort of Internet access.

If I'm expecting a specific letter, or if my friend sees mail coming in that looks as if I might need to read it, I've given her permission to open any mail and e-mail me the contents or whatever I need to know.

I don't change the message on my answering machine, nor do I pick up voice mail messages while on the road. I don't want to alert callers that I'm not home, and anyone who needs me that badly can e-mail me.

How to protect your rig in the winter

In order to keep the pipes from freezing (and breaking), I take my RV to my friendly RV service people for winterizing. They empty all the tanks and put a special RV antifreeze (it's pink and frothy and isn't poisonous) in the pipes. The rig then sleeps happily in the backyard until spring, when I take it back to be "summerized," by which I mean getting the antifreeze out of the pipes, as well as checking/changing the oil, wipers, tire pressure, and so forth.

Recently I've discovered I can minimize insurance coverage on my RV during the winter. When I'm ready to get back on the road again, a phone call to my agent renews full coverage.

After eight years of paying someone to jumpstart the rig in the spring, I finally learned to plug it into the house power with an outside outlet. That keeps the coach batteries fully charged through the long, cold winter. In the spring, when the engine battery won't start, I push a MOM switch.

"Why does my RV have a mama switch?" I asked my service people plaintively, back when I was young and ignorant. It stands for MOMentary power, or auxiliary power, and allows the engine battery to draw power from the coach batteries in order to start the engine. The service guy explained this very nicely—after he stopped laughing.

Can I use my rig in the winter? Yes, even if the temperature is going to stay below freezing, as long as I'm careful about water. I set up a trip to Phoenix one Thanksgiving, though it never actually happened. I would tape over the sink drains, giving me a visual reminder not to pour anything in the sink. I would dump my Coke® residue on the ground and brush my teeth over the toilet. I planned to flush the toilet with bottled water, adding RV antifreeze for the mountains where the temperature was low. Another possibility would have been to just use the RV normally and have it re-winterized when I got home. However, those cold mountain passes could have caused major trouble, and this seemed the simpler solution. When the furnace is on, the pipes will not freeze even in winter. On the road, though.... I have also discovered that most RVs are not insulated sufficiently to keep out freezing wind.

How to do laundry on the road

Most campgrounds offer laundry facilities. Frequently the dial-up computer access is in the laundry room, giving me something to do while I wait. Since the washer and dryer happily consume large numbers of quarters, I've learned to get change before the store closes. Rather than pay for expensive miniature boxes of detergent, I carry detergent tablets or pour measured amounts into zipper bags at home and carry them with me.

I've learned the hard way to scrutinize the washer and dryer before putting my clothes in. You wouldn't believe the things people do in public laundries!

How to go grocery shopping

Well, pretty much the way you shop at home.

I do park on the outskirts of the lot, taking up four spaces in order to ensure my ability to leave later.

I watch for stores where I have a club, membership, or discount card. Your card may work, even if the name of the store is different (City Market, King Soopers, Kroger, and many others are all affiliated, for example, and accept each other's cards).

Isn't gas awfully expensive?

Oh my, yes! Since gas pumps automatically shut off at a predetermined amount of money (generally $50, $75, or $100), I have to swipe my card three or four times before my 65-gallon tank is full. After twice, the pump freezes; then I go in and explain, "I'm the RV out there at pump 3. Want to clear the display for me?" I leave my card and return to the pump, paying inside. Of course, it would be simpler to pay inside from the start, but my card company offers a discount for gas purchases at the pump.

How do I justify the expense, you are wondering? Well, I'm paying $25-$35 a night at a campground, instead of hotel/motel prices. I'm cooking my own food, instead of paying restaurant prices. I have my pets with me, instead of paying for a kennel.

All in all, I tend to come out ahead. And I sure do have fun!

Tools: Checklists for Outside and Inside Walk-Arounds

Checklist for the outside walk-around
____ all hoses and cords stored safely
____ awning put away
____ all storage bays (the "basement") latched securely
____ step put in (if it isn't automatic)
____ slide-out in
____ stove vent closed
____ nothing on the picnic table
____ nothing hanging from the trees
____ nothing lying on the grass/cement/gravel/whatever
____ one full circuit of the RV without seeing anything that needs to be taken care of

Checklist for the inside walk-around
____ water tank levels checked—black, gray, and fresh
____ enough propane
____ enough gasoline
____ slide-out in
____ antenna down
____ furnace or AC off
____ water heater off
____ water pump on
____ fridge packed safely so things don't spill or break
____ fridge set to automatic (or gas) so it will work when you disconnect
____ all cabinet doors and drawers closed securely
____ all surfaces free of things that will slide or roll
____ laptop computer and printer in a safe place
____ doors latched (open or closed) so they won't flap and slam
____ vents closed
____ beds and bedding put away
____ trash taken out or stored away
____ pet water dish secure and filled
____ seatbelts fastened (for your passengers—and remember to fasten yours, too)
____ door locked

Travel Is Pretty Simple
Six TIPS for Dealing with Maintenance Emergencies

1. File notes from your walk-through at the time of purchase with your manuals.
2. Keep all those notes and manuals handy.
3. Ask questions when you're getting service: talk to the salesman, your service guys, tow truck drivers, other RVers.
4. Be prepared:
    a. Have flashlights in the RV.
    b. Use gloves and wear washable shoes when dumping holding tanks.
    c. Keep at least half a tank of gas at all times.
5. Have extra quilts for unexpectedly cold nights
6. Have wet wipes available.

Travel Is Pretty Simple
Nine TIPS for Using Your Mirrors

1. Set the driver's seat comfortably for the main driver first.
2. Don't try to adjust mirrors alone; have a helper outside the rig.
3. You should have two mirrors on each side: a regular, flat one; a curved, "spot" one.
4. Adjust each flat mirror
    a. So you can see just the edge of the side of the rig
    b. So you can see the lane next to you quite a way behind the rig
    c. So you can see the bottom back corner of the rig and the rear tire touching the road surface
    d. So you can see the lane marker stripe
5. Adjust each spot mirror
    a. So you can see just the edge of the side of the rig
    b. So you can see the lane next to you the length of the rig
    c. So you can see the bottom, back corner of the rig and the rear tire touching the road surface
    d. So you can see the lane marker stripe
6. Drive within the lane marker stripes; try to stay centered.
7. Don't change lanes if your spot mirror shows a vehicle.
8. Remember that your tail swings out when you turn.
    a. Watch your corners
    b. Note where your rear tires are in relation to curbs and other hazards
    c. Try to turn from an outside lane
9. Many truckers will flash their lights when it's safe to pull in front of them when passing or changing lanes on the highway.
    a. If that's helpful to you, do it for other drivers, too.
    b. Blink your parking lights a couple of times to thank them.

Travel Is Pretty Simple
Six TIPS for Converting to and from Metric

1. Use a conversion tool when you're planning:
    (http://www.psinvention.com/zoetic/convert.htm)
    a. There are other Web sites available, also.
    b. Visitor Centers near the border may have a conversion table for you.
2. Distance
    a. Indicate on your itinerary whether mileage is metric or American.
    b. Automobile speedometers are marked in both metric and American.
    c. Use your speedometer as a rough converter (since 50 mph=80 kph, then 50 miles is 80 km).
    d. For short distances, a meter and a yard are about equivalent
3. Money
    a. Ask at the border for the current exchange rate, which varies widely, even from day to day.
    b. Figure a simple and rough conversion so you can think about prices in stores ("about half" or "about one-and-a-half").
4. Gas
    a. Remember, English and metric gallons are not the same size.
    b. There are about 4 liters to an English gallon.
    c. I find it simplest not to try to convert liters/gallon to miles/gallon; there are too many variables.
5. Temperature
    a. The United States thinks in Fahrenheit (F). Canada thinks in Celsius (C).
    b. 5/9 (F-32)=C (subtract 32 from the Fahrenheit temperature; multiply the answer by 5/9). For a VERY ROUGH equivalent: F-30, take half of it (subtract 30 from the F temperature, then take half of that).
    c. (9/5 C) + 32 = F (multiply the Celsius temperature by 9/5, then add 32). For a VERY ROUGH equivalent: Twice C and add 30.
6. Your RV
    a. You may need to know your vehicle's height, width, and weight in metric.
    b. Your vehicle's data sticker will have the data listed both ways.
    c. Know your height and width without having to check when you come upon narrow lanes, overpasses, and so forth.

Chapter 5: Historical Perspective
The Reluctant Draggin'

Back in the Olden Days of Trailering

Once upon a time, this is what trailering was like ...

"I have a new game," I told my group of special needs second graders. They all had problems with focus, coordination, and academics. I had discovered our reading lessons went better if we started each session with some repeated, rhythmic activities.

"It's a clapping game," I went on. "I learned it when I was a girl, back when the dinosaurs were around."

I paused, waiting for laughter or, at least, a smile or quizzical look. They stared solemnly at me.

"Hey, guys, are you listening?"

Heads nodded.

"Well, did I just say something for true? Or did I say something silly?"

They considered this.

"You said true," Willem said.

"Yeah, it was true," Davie agreed.

"Teachers have to tell the truth," Trent stated firmly.

Carlos looked up at me through uncombed hair.

"You were being silly!" he said positively.

"Oh, good listening, Carlos! You're right! I said something silly. What did I say that was silly, Carlos?"

Carlos leaned over and flicked me on the shoulder with his finger. It was an oddly flirtatious gesture. He giggled.

"You said you used to be a girl!"

Well, back when I was a girl, in Webster Groves, a suburb of St. Louis, Missouri, my parents and I car-camped. My parents put a tarp over the open back of Susie Blue, our station wagon, and slept there. I slept on the front seat. We cooked on a Coleman stove or over a campfire.

Then, as my mother wrote a friend, we made a major change:

Feb. 22, 1956
Our latest family project is the purchase of a trailer. Yes, believe it or not, a house trailer. Everyone thinks we're out of our minds,

and none of our friends can summon up any more enthusiasm than merely being happy we're happy—last thing in the world any one of them would want! But all three of us are slightly batty with joy over the whole undertaking.

It's a little one (when we start pulling it I imagine we'll think it's enormous, but it's just 19 feet) with just room for all of us to sleep comfortably, a cute kitchen, and lots of closets and storage space. No luxuries like a bathroom—we're not planning to retire in it or anything, just move from place to place on vacations.

We used blocks of ice in the fridge. Did you know a Coke bottle will melt its way into a block of ice, which will then freeze around it? There's nothing like a truly ice-cold Coke to quench your thirst on a hot day.

We played "Friend or Foe" as we drove, honking and waving whenever we passed another trailer and keeping track of the responses. These sightings were few, except when we were in the Far West; then we saw Airstreams from California. Most were friends, honking and waving back. Almost every evening tenters would knock on our door: "May I see what it looks like inside?"

We had that old Masonite® trailer just a year when the car swerved on an open stretch of highway. The trailer started swinging, and soon it was on its side on the wrong side of the road, with the car on its roof. This was well before the days of seatbelts, but no one was injured.

My parents had a shiny new trailer built. It had a real refrigerator and lights that worked with shore power or battery, but still no bathroom facilities.

Mother carefully painted a red dragon on the back of the trailer. Then she stenciled *The Reluctant Draggin'* below the picture—a pun on Kenneth Grahame's *Reluctant Dragon*—because the trailer was *Draggin'* along behind us. We were mentioned in the *Reader's Digest* in 1958: "Seen on a trailer in Texas: Trailer with *Reluctant Draggin'* on back." Mother framed the page.

My parents upgraded again when I was in college. The new *Draggin'* had air conditioning, a radio, and both toilet and shower. Mother's multiple sclerosis made traveling more difficult, but being able to carry the machines and medication that kept her going allowed them to continue to enjoy driving to Indiana to see the colorful leaves of the Midwest each fall, and to Land Between the Lakes (Kentucky-Tennessee) for the blooming redbud and dogwood each spring.

Because of my summers in the *Draggin'*, I knew an RV lifestyle would work for me—and it has.

Chapter 6: Your RV Toolbox
How Do You Organize All Your Stuff?

Did You Pack the Cat Food?

Not everyone will want to organize the same way,
but this is how I do it.

My canine navigator starts getting excited when I get out the baskets to pack the RV. Her tail flies back and forth, with the cat batting at it in delighted incomprehension.

Of course, Lady has gone on all my RV trips. She knows those piles of underwear and shorts mean that soon we will be driving down the highway and pulling off at rest areas, campgrounds, and zoo parking lots where—bliss!—there will be people waiting to pat her.

Dolphin doesn't choose to figure out what I'm doing. To him, baskets are something to curl up in or, if they are full, to tip over and then dart away, laughing his silent feline laugh.

I, on the other hand, am filling the baskets according to a basic list, modified for each trip. I keep the list on my computer, adding and deleting depending on when and where I'm going. Will I be attending a wedding? I add dress clothes and shoes. Is it still April? I can cross off the swimsuit.

Clothing

My RV has few drawers except in the kitchen, so I fill inexpensive plastic baskets and store them in the overhead storage areas. It is easy to kneel on the bed, flip up the door, and pull out my clothes for the day. The closet has blouses, an outfit for church, and "weather clothing": raincoat, heavy sweater, and my winter coat (with gloves and scarf, just in case).

I choose clothing that is comfortable, does not need to be ironed, and requires no special treatment when washed. I pack one pair of extra all-purpose shoes for when my feet are tired, plus sandals and water shoes (for both wading and showering).

Dirty clothes sit in a corner in a laundry bag, each day becoming a softer beagle cushion until I ruin the effect by doing the laundry some evening in a campground. (The purpose behind this activity escapes Lady completely.) After folding and putting away the clean clothes, I toss a detergent tablet into the laundry bag, and we're ready for another week.

Food and kitchen supplies

Most things can be purchased at any grocery store along the road. I shop in advance for items that might be available only locally, primarily pet food and the bedtime snacks that help maintain my blood sugar level. On my Alaska trip a few years ago, I was startled to learn I cannot buy frozen egg dishes in Canadian grocery stores; now I stock up before crossing the border.

Kitchen basics—dishes, flatware, cooking utensils, coffee, instant cocoa, and non-perishable snacks—stay in the RV year-round. Anything that should not be frozen, such as pancake syrup and canned soup, is taken out in the fall and returned for the first trip of the spring. I lug only refrigerator/freezer foods from house to RV and back during the summer. I use an expandable bar in the fridge to keep things from sliding or tipping as I drive.

Lady and Dolphin's food stays in an outside storage bin, except for the package I'm currently using. Lady makes sure her treats are stowed away before we leave. She knows precisely which drawer they are in and expects something whenever that drawer is opened. Every time I open a cabinet door, Dolphin rushes in, hoping to find something exciting. He cannot decide which is more fun, to curl up and nap in a cabinet, or to push things out onto the floor.

Miscellaneous

In addition to hanging clothes, the closet has cleaning supplies (vacuum and broom) and a box with all the manuals I got with the RV. My books are shelved in a cabinet. Reference books—a dictionary as well as tree, flower, reptile, and animal identification guides—remain permanently in the RV. I start each trip with a few intriguing paperbacks, knowing I will find books to buy (or, at some campgrounds, trade) along the way. Dolphin enjoys slipping in to rearrange them. A deft push with a paw can produce a truly awesome crash. Books that escape from the restraining bar have a habit of sliding all over the place, even without Dolphin's help.

Books on tape are generally in a basket behind the driver's seat. And I do mean on tape, not on CD. With tape, I am able to eject the book, listen to something else, and return later to where I left off.

I have a backseat organizer (designed to keep crayons and travel games organized for a child) hanging on the side of the passenger seat. Dolphin noses into it, hoping for … what, I wonder, perhaps a mouse? All he finds, however, are tour books and maps, piled chronologically.

Dolphin's litter box lives in the shower stall, with a baby gate to keep the dog out. The spill-proof water dish is tucked on the floor in a corner, on a non-skid mat.

Vitamins, first aid supplies, and toiletries go in smaller baskets that fit in the bathroom cabinet. Though I move my clothing back to the house after each trip, the bathroom baskets stay until the end of the season. I tried keeping them permanently in the RV but discovered shampoo and deodorant do not take kindly to being frozen.

I have one drawer dedicated to essential tools: my phone charger, battery charger, an alarm clock (not really needed with Dolphin and Lady around), duct tape, extra batteries, a screwdriver.

My double bed has extra room, even with the three of us stretched out on it, so my laptop, Bible, a book, and my CPAP machine (Continuous Positive Air Pressure, which helps me breathe at night; I have sleep apnea) line the edge of the bed by the wall.

When I've packed the last-minute items (toothbrush, CPAP machine, litter box), I scoop up Dolphin, tell Lady, "Let's go to the RV!" and happily lock the house door behind me. We're off!

Tools for Packing

- Keep your packing list on your computer
- Adapt it to the specific needs of each trip, then print it out
- Check items off as you pack them
- Make sure you easily get at things you will use often
- Pack children's clothes within their reach
- Buy enough baskets or containers to keep things together
- Remember clothes for potential bad weather
- Provide clothes for special occasions.
  - o   dress shoes and underwear
  - o   coat or jacket
- Store everything securely, so it won't slide around and get lost
- Have bathroom and laundry supplies portable

Tool: Sample Packing List

Clothes

slacks (2)	long-sleeve shirt (1-2)	coat
hat	warm hat	gloves
shorts (3-4)	blouses (7)	underwear (7)
socks (7)	spare shoes	raincoat
sweater	windbreaker	sweatshirt
swim suit	water shoes	

Personal

Bible	daily Bible reading guide	books
hymnal, songs	CDs	tapes
books on tape	laptop	printer
paper	adaptor	phone cord
e-mail addresses	postcard addresses	stamps
cameras (4)	film	

RV	pharm &	food
itinerary	toothbrush	cocoa
maps	toothpaste	health bars
tour guides	deodorant	breakfasts
campground guides	shampoo	chicken
passport	rinse	suppers
car reg. etc.	brush	ice cream
towels	sunblock	fruit
bedding	pain spray	yogurt
sheets	itch stuff	Coke, Diet Rite®
comforters	1st aid kit	Emergen-C®
pillows	Tums	juice mix
seat cushion	immodium	water bottle
back rest	ibuprofen	veggies
bungies	eye drops	
phone		

pets		TO DO	
dog food	litter liners	get trav ✓s	transfer files to laptop
cat food	dog treats	get cash	
leash	flea/tick stuff	itinerary to friend	
litter box	heart worm med	cancel papers	
health cert.	vet contact info	arrange for mail	

<u>*Travel Is Pretty Simple*</u>
<u>Four TIPS for Major Essentials</u>

1. Make sure shower supplies are separable, portable, and clean.
   a. Color code toothbrushes and towels, or color code the baskets they're in.
   b. Each person should have their own, easily identifiable shower basket or tote.
   c. Soap should be in a soapbox; toothbrushes in a cover.
2. Install extra hooks or towels racks for drying towels, swim suits, and so forth.
3. Take any special food you must have—personal passions and addictions, comfort food, food for motion sickness, …
4. Pack comfort books (kids and adults alike) and reference books (concordance, flower and animal identification, …).

Chapter 7: Side Trip to Yosemite National Park, California July, 2006

I Had It All Together

Even with good organization, odd things happen.

I had to admit it was beautiful, the Yosemite KOA, but it was so steep! Of course, it was part of the mountain range; that was the source of its charm. But I was camped at the bottom of the slope, the facilities were at the top, and my hip ached.

I ate my breakfast and watched the cat chase a camp-robber jay from window to window, until the clatter of an early-morning trash pickup scared them both.

Dolphin leapt to the table next to me, where he nonchalantly licked his toes, explaining he hadn't *really* been frightened; he was just getting bored with the game.

"You're a big, brave tiger-boy," I told him comfortingly. I scratched under his chin, pulled my hand back quickly to avoid being nipped, and moved on with my morning routine.

I planned to take the trash with me when I showered, to avoid climbing the hill twice. My shower basket is about five by seven by three, with a handle. It holds shampoo, soap in a soapbox, and deodorant. I added my hairbrush and washcloth, tossed my towels over my arm, tucked my keys in my pocket, and picked up the trash bag.

"You guys be good!" I called as I headed up the hill, step after painful step.

The dumpster had a heavy metal lid, and my two-finger push could not budge it. I transferred the trash bag to my other hand and managed to get the lid up. Bracing it with my elbow on the edge of the bin, I swung my left hand up and through the opening. As my fingers released their hold, I realized what was about to happen—but it was too late to change my action. I watched in distress as the bag of trash plummeted to the bottom of the empty dumpster, closely followed by my shower basket.

Time slowed, and a part of me wondered whether I would swear or cry. Instead, somewhat to my surprise, I laughed.

"I could have had my keys in the basket!" I told myself as I trudged back down the hill. "Or my watch. There's really no harm done."

And I added *shampoo, soap, brush, deodorant,* and *washcloth* to my shopping list before disconnecting and driving north on I-5 to check out Lassen Volcanic National Park. There I was so enthralled with the historical photos of the actual eruption that I forgot my greasy hair completely.

Chapter 8: Historical Perspective
Father's Day, 1959

Not a Packing Problem

We thought we were so organized!

"Elsi, we'll be traveling on Father's Day! What will we do?"

I looked at my mother in surprise. Out of town for Father's Day? That hadn't happened before—at least, not in my twelve-year-old memory. I thought a moment.

"Well, we'll bring his presents and cards, and give them to him at breakfast that morning. He'll be really surprised! That'll be fun!"

"But how can we hide the presents, where Daddy won't find them, I mean?" Mother asked.

"I'll put them under my socks and stuff, in the back of my clothing shelf," I said confidently. "He'll never look in there."

So that's what we did. I made Daddy a card and bought him a present. Mother gave me her things, and I slipped them into the back of my shelf. Each of us had one shelf for all our clothes, except for coats and shoes, of course. Mother and Daddy sometimes looked in each other's shelves, but nobody bothered mine. It was too low for them to get at comfortably, and they didn't worry about my clothes, anyway. So it was a great hiding place. I often had chocolate bars tucked away there, ready for surreptitious midnight snacks.

This wasn't a real vacation. Those were six weeks long and covered a quarter of the country. This was just a two-week jaunt, up to Minnesota to visit Uncle Mace and Aunt Helen, and my cousin Pete. He was a college boy, and I thought he was wonderful.

We had a good trip, stopping to visit Paul Bunyan in Brainerd, cooking burgers on the shore of Lake Superior, wearing borrowed black-and-red-checked lumberman's shirts against the wind off the lake. Pete let me tag after him and treated me like a real person, almost like an adult!

We pulled into the driveway a little after 3:00 Sunday afternoon. Daddy worked on parking the trailer and getting unhitched. Mother emptied the fridge and gathered clothes and dishes to be washed. I brought in the newspaper and curled up on the sofa with the comics.

Hm, something odd about the funnies today ... they're all about ... oh!

I jumped up and ran to the trailer.

"'Scuse me, Daddy. I just have to get something!"

I burrowed in my clothing shelf, pulling out an armload of clothes ... and the presents.

We celebrated Father's Day at supper, at home. It had been a good idea, anyway.

The *Reluctant Draggin'* was the first travel trailer my family had. Mother painted the dragon on the back in 1957.

The *Travelin' Tortoise* was my first RV, providing a safe "turtle shell" for me to retreat to. It is parked in front of my house in 1998.

Lady takes her duties in the navigator's seat seriously. However, I think she should be checking the map and watching for exit signs, while she wants to be sure she is well rested to greet beagle-patters at our next stop.

Dolphin is apparently paying attention during his shift in the navigator's seat.

→ *PART 2: PLANNING*

Chapter 9: Your RV Toolbox
Your Personal Vacation Style

Watching the Ants or Being Patted

Knowing how you like to travel will help you plan.

My navigator's travel style is clear: She doesn't like rainy days, because she doesn't like getting her paws wet. She prefers I drive with cruise control on, because it lulls her to sleep. She wants to drive east, because the time zone change means she gets supper earlier. And her main purpose for a walk is to find people who will pat her.

The cat's style is almost opposite—which fits his contrary personality. He wants to sit in the grass and look for ants, blowing leaves, or low-flying birds. He loves driving on rainy days, because he can chase the windshield wipers.

They both like drive-through meals, Lady because she gets a bite, and Dolphin because he can play with the straw when I'm done with it (or sooner, if I get distracted). Of course, I don't actually drive through—sometimes I can drive by the order box and shout my order, then park by the window, get out, and pick it up. But most of the time I park, go in, and take the food back to my eager family. At a Chick-Fil-A® in the Northwest, the manager noticed my two sweet, furry faces pressed against the screens and asked, "May I buy them a box of chicken bites?" They were grateful.

When I started out in my first RV, I thought I knew my own vacation style preferences. When I was a child, we hiked, went on tours, and read all the explanatory signs in museums. We were busy from breakfast to bedtime, either being tourists or driving from activity to activity, carefully avoiding "tacky tourist traps." That, therefore, was the type of itinerary I planned when I bought my first RV. I made campground reservations in advance, planned activities or driving for after supper, and filled my days with busy-ness.

A few weeks' experience showed me that I like being up with the dawn (except in Alaska) for a morning walk with Lady, a shower, and a leisurely start to the morning. I like stopping when I see something interesting, taking time to admire the scenery or write a poem, and finding a campground when I am getting tired. I enjoy having time in the evening to write about the day's activities on my laptop, check information for the following day, and go to bed early. Lady curls up next to me, Dolphin lies purring on my stomach, and I read and snack until we all fall asleep.

Before you can plan a viable itinerary, you need to know your personal traveling style, as well as the preferences of anyone you're traveling with. Here are some issues to consider:

➜ Do you have just one or two main objectives, or do you want to sightsee along the way? And, do you want to see everything available at each stop, or just hit the high points?

One set of friends decided they could drive the approximately 1,700 miles to Washington, D.C. in three days. With three more days to cover D.C., they could head to Philadelphia to see the Liberty Bell, drop by Niagara Falls, and still make it back home in less than two weeks.

I, on the other hand, like to stop for every oddity I can find, including the UFO water tower in Ogallala, Nebraska … the geographic center of North America near Rugby, North Dakota … and the world's largest pheasant in Huron, South Dakota. I don't make great time, but I do have fun!

➜ Do you want to keep moving, or would you prefer to set up camp for several days at a time?

I want to see things and drive on. Only when visiting friends or at national parks do I stay more than one night in the same place. I camped two nights at Glacier National Park before moving on, but I did spend almost a week at Yellowstone—and saw a dozen bears on one full-day tour!

My traveling friend Diane, however, would be perfectly content, to camp in each place for a week. She wants to sit for hours in a flowered field or by a brook. She would love to visit every museum in each park, read every sign, and photograph every scenic overlook.

Which is better? It's a matter of personal preference.

➜ Do you need a detailed list of goals and activities each day, a general plan for the trip with plenty of flexibility, or a totally open span of time to see what comes up?

"Let's plan!" my father would say. We then sat down with AAA guides and maps. He wrote out a day-by-day itinerary, with the activities of each day listed and about how long each would take. No extra train ride or unexpected road hazard was allowed to interfere with the plan.

I write an itinerary but am happy to diverge from it.

➜ What amenities are essential for overnight stops? Think about hookups for your rig, access to cable TV or modem connection, a swimming pool, a game room, trail rides, and so forth.

I spend about a week each summer traveling with Diane and her two children. We commit to one trail ride and some sort of animal encounter for each trip; this satisfies the children. We carve out time for my friend to sit by a stream and pray or daydream alone. We make sure there is a swimming pool at each night stop (for the kids) and modem accessibility (for me).

→ What sorts of activities do you want to participate in when you stop? Do you like museums? Organized tours? Hiking? Rafting? Biking? Scenery? Silly things, such as Carhenge (a Nebraska copy of Stonehenge built from junked cars)?

Allow each participant to choose one special activity. Don't worry about what your friends or family will think about your choices; just enjoy them.

→ Are you flexible enough to change your plans if something more interesting comes along?

Driving down the Parks Highway from Fairbanks to Anchorage, Alaska, I startled my friends by suddenly swerving into a parking lot. I had spotted a reindeer on a leash, and we spent a delightful half-hour petting him.

Another summer, I committed to visiting a friend in Mitchell, South Dakota, Tuesday morning but arrived three days early. A visit to Cabela's, a trip to a Laura Ingalls Wilder site, and several dog walks filled the spare time nicely and gave me a rest.

Knowing your travel preferences, as well as those of your traveling companions, helps make every trip a keeper, with memories and pictures you will treasure forever. When you know in advance that your companions will need time at the mall, for example, or have no intention of stopping for lunch … when you know you won't rest until you've checked email in the evening … you are better able to plan for your own needs as well as theirs. And having some of these matters figured out ahead of time lessens your stress level—always a good thing.

Tools for Figuring Out Your Vacation Style

What's your preference?
- Important objectives OR sightseeing along the way
- See everything available at each stop OR just the high points
- Keep moving OR set up camp for several days
- Detailed list of goals and activities OR general plan for the trip with flexibility OR open span of time
- LIST amenities essential for overnight stops
- LIST activities to participate in when you stop
- Are you flexible enough to change your plans if something more interesting comes along?

Chapter 10: Side Trip to Estes Park, Colorado
Labor Day weekend, 2003

Why Are We Here?

Don't miss the obvious when you plan your trip.

"Where are you from?" I asked the woman in front of me. There was quite a line for the campground showers.

She shifted her grip on her towels and answered, "Nebraska. We came in for the Denver Flea Market."

"You drove to Estes Park on Labor Day weekend for a flea market in Denver?" I failed to keep the surprise out of my voice, and she looked at me in confusion.

"Sure! What are you here for?"

"Well, this morning we're driving Trail Ridge Road."

"What's that?" The question came from behind me in line.

"It's the highest paved road in the United States," I answered. "It's just over there, in the park." I waved vaguely, wondering which way west was.

"So it's right here in Estes Park?" the first woman asked.

"No, in Rocky Mountain National Park."

"Where's that?"

Taken aback, I tried to explain about Estes Park being a town, the gateway to Rocky Mountain National Park. I was glad when my turn to shower came and I could leave the conversation.

Later that day, at Fall River Pass, 11,796 feet above sea level, I gazed at the layers of mountains and laughed.

"Lord, what they're missing!" I whispered as I picked up my camera. I had come for this view of one of the prime sections of God's creation. And I planned to enjoy every moment. *Wow!*

Chapter 11: Your RV Toolbox
Making an Itinerary

Where Shall We Go?

How I build my itinerary

Tolkien told us, "The road goes ever on and on." You could keep going on the roads, without repeating, almost forever. It is, after all, a big continent, and there are 830 highways in the United States alone.

So the question becomes, where do you want to go? Which will be influenced, of course, by how long you have and what other commitments you might have made.

"Let's plan!" my father would say. And out would come maps, tour guides, and notebooks. His idea was to spend about six weeks covering a quarter of the continent on each trip. We didn't repeat activities and preferred main roads, which focused our planning nicely.

I, on the other hand, start my planning with the purpose for my trip. If it's "just" my vacation, for relaxation, then I can dream big: Maine, Alaska, … but some of my favorite trips have started with a single, short-term goal: a wedding, an errand, a graduation.

Once I at least have a direction, I read travel guides. Because I'm a AAA member, that's where I start, as the books are free and comprehensive. But I've developed a collection of commercial tourbooks I can refer to, as well as RV and area magazines. I talk to friends, check the Internet, and read my parents' logs of my childhood trips, too.

As I read, I highlight everything that sounds attractive. Later I mark those places on state maps. Usually I see either a clump of high-interest sites close together or a wandering line of connect-the-dots roads, easy to turn into a route.

Evolving itineraries

One spring, I had been invited to a nephew's college graduation. *If I'm driving all the way from Colorado to South Carolina*, I thought, *I might as well duck up to Virginia to visit a high school friend. And, if I'm that far from home, what else is there for me to do or see?* My final itinerary included the geographic center of the United States (north central Kansas), the St. Louis Zoo's new puffin/penguin center, Land Between the Lakes (Kentucky/Tennessee border), Great Smoky Mountain

National Park, and the Blue Ridge Parkway. I ended up back in Colorado just in time for the Colorado Christian Writers Conference in Estes Park.

Another jaunt started with a wedding in St. Louis. It turned into a three-week author tour, covering Laura Ingalls Wilder's adult home in Mansfield, Missouri, Gene Stratton Porter's home in Geneva, Indiana, and Bess Streeter Aldrich's house in Elmwood, Nebraska. I took my treasured copies of the *Little House* books, *Freckles, Girl of the Limberlost*, and *Lantern in Her Hand* to re-read along the way. That was the trip I discovered the Indiana Sand Dunes, just off Lake Michigan.

On my way to retrieve a friend's son from his Oklahoma college, I was able to stop by a nephew's high school graduation and visit friends in Missouri. I enjoyed the rivers in the Missouri Ozarks and found some intriguing rock formations, too.

Timeline

Once I know where I would go if I only had I "world enough and time," as Andrew Marvel puts it, I build a rough timeline. On my own, with no planned stops, I average 50-60 mph (that is, I drive interstate speeds but stop frequently for food and to stretch my legs). So 400 miles is a pleasant driving day for me, though I've done up to twelve road hours (about 700 miles) with a pressing deadline and books on tape to keep me awake and focused.

I plug in time for stops—the AAA guidebooks often have recommended ranges. Area guides also suggest length of stay; for example, four-and-a-half hours for the St. Louis Zoo. Other time constraints are related to the attraction itself—a train that leaves at 10 or 2, a museum that's closed on Mondays. And I want to be in church Sundays, which shortens that day.

As the pieces fall together, I make other choices. That train is interesting, but it's half a state away from anything else I'm doing; save it for another trip. This road sounds terrible, so I'll allow extra time.

Why do I bother with an itinerary at all? I've missed activities I cared about by arriving on a closed day, too late for a once-a-day activity, or without having changed my watch at a time zone line. Time zones can be confusing, by the way. For example, crossing from Alberta to Saskatchewan, you move into the Central Time Zone; however, they don't do daylight saving time, so the time doesn't really change until you cross into Manitoba.

"I've never been to Alaska," I thought one year. That summer, I drove the Fossil Trail in Canada as well as the Alaska-Canada Highway. I took train trips, went on a couple of short cruises, and crossed the Arctic Circle. I even got to pat a moose—which turns out not to be worth the trouble, other than the glory of having done it. Lady got to bark at it, also, although the highlight of the trip for her was midnight walks under the setting sun.

So, where do you want to go? What can you do and see on the way there and back again? What plans will build the best memories in the time you have available?

Tools for Planning an Itinerary

Ask yourself:
- Where am I going and why?
- How long can I be out, and how far can I go in a day?
- Have I read tour books to see what's along the way?
- Have I allowed time for extras, flat tires, laundry, and weather problems?
- Does everyone in the family have something they really want to do?

See Appendix B: Resource Materials for information on tour guidebooks.

Travel Is Pretty Simple
Eight TIPS for Web Sites Listing Odd or Large Things to See

1. Large Canadian Roadside Attractions: Trans-Canada Highway
   http://www.roadsideattractions.ca/tch.htm
2. Roadside America: Guide to Uniquely Odd Tourist Attractions
   http://www.roadsideamerica.com/
3. World's Largest Roadside Attractions
   http://www.wlra.us/
4. World's Largest Things Traveling Roadside Attraction
   http://www.worldslargestthings.com/
5. Canada, Home to Large Roadside Attractions
   http://www.buzzle.com/editorials/7-5-2005-72661.asp
6. 59 Jaw-Dropping Roadside Attractions: Southwest
   http://budgettravelonline.com/bt-dyn/content/article/2006/06/05/
   AR2006060500673.html
7. Wikipedia: Roadside Attractions
   http://en.wikipedia.org/wiki/Roadside_attraction
8. 43 Places: Interesting Places in Your City
   http://www.43places.com/

Chapter 12: Trip Commentary
Planning Your Worst Trip Ever

"Warning, Will Robinson!"

Don't do these, and you'll be fine.

Choose your destination by considering places you will be proud to tell others about, places that will give the children extra credit in their schoolwork next year, or places that people you want to impress have mentioned as being important.

Plan to leave on a Friday after work, or the morning after school closes. If this is not possible, pick a date that causes you to miss an event important to someone you care about. This will ensure that everyone will be crabby as you drive out, and that something essential will have been forgotten in the frantic, last-minute attempt to pack everything.

Forget about a "shake-down cruise"—a weekend trip to discover problems or concerns with the RV. Rinse the antifreeze out of the pipes and take off for six weeks in the outback.

Mis-figure your daily mileage, or over-plan how far you can go in a day. This will cut out unimportant bathroom or meal stops and keep you on the road long after everyone's bedtime.

Leave foul-weather clothes homes, so the unseasonable blizzard or clammy rainstorm will add interest to planned activities.

Make no advance reservations for tours and special events. Instead, talk those activities up so the family is excited about them, ensuring major meltdowns when it turns out there are no tickets available.

Ignore candy factories, zoos, or outlet stores not in your plans, no matter how enticing the signs.

Disregard personal needs and limitations. Plan a five-mile cave tour if you have arthritis, a trip to Disney World with a colicky baby, a whale-watch cruise if your daughter gets seasick easily.

Forget to factor in time for laundry, shopping, upset stomachs, or the occasional flat tire. This simple step alone can add hours of stress to an otherwise bland trip.

Carry only a single, expensive camera. Drop it in the lake or on the rocks, or accidentally open the back in mid-roll. Have no spares packed. If using a video camera, make a point of staring into the lens muttering, "Is this thing on?" Be sure to turn the camera on before twisting from side to side to find the best angle for a shot. Run out of film just before Mickey Mouse, a beluga whale, or Old Faithful appears.

A few days before the end of the trip, start making comments about how you're never going on another vacation again, people are so inconsiderate, and why is there always construction on the roads you are on?

Invite neighbors and family members over to see your slides, photos, or video-tape. Give long explanations of each scene, making remarks about problems along the way. If you are showing digital pictures, arrange for the computer to crash just before the doorbell rings.

Chapter 13: Side Trip to Waterloo, Iowa
July 1958; October 2006

No Spot Is So Dear to My Childhood

Just a little trip, filled with lots of good memories!

"Small detour to view site of Daddy's favorite hymn, 'Little Brown Church,'" says my parents' trip log from July, 1958. "Discovered it's Congregational. Daddy brazenly plugged in their P.A. system so we could sit in the pew and hear the proper atmospheric music."

My father was not noted for his ability to carry a tune. He could manage the rhythm, but major changes in the notes were beyond him. In fact, one Christmas our neighborhood caroling group specialized in "The Little Drummer Boy." Daddy and two similarly tone-deaf men provided a wonderful "pa rum pa pum pum" backdrop.

"Little Brown Church" was a favorite song of his. Mother and I did the verses in two-part harmony, and Daddy picked up with the "Oh, come, come, come, come" counter-part on the chorus.

What fun to discover the actual church, nestled in Iowa's green hills. Unlikely as it seems to me, the song was written before the church was built; the builders hadn't heard the song and used brown paint because it was cheap. We didn't know this when I visited as a child. I Googled the site before visiting as an adult and was fascinated by the story.

Barely 80 miles away is a "lost" *Little House* site. Laura Ingalls Wilder's family lived in Burr Oak between *On the Banks of Plum Creek* and *By the Shores of Silver Lake*. Cynthia Rylant used Wilder's notes to write *Old Town in the Green Groves* about this time in Laura Ingalls Wilder's life.

So, as I drive through Iowa, I sing the songs of my childhood:

> *No spot is so dear to my childhood*
> *As the little brown church in the vale!*
>
> "Little Brown Church in the Vale," William Pitts

Chapter 14: Side Trip to Resurrection Bay, Alaska
July 2002

Visiting the Land of the Giants

Before or during your trip,
you may discover fascinating bits of information.

Remember *Gulliver's Travels*? Most of us know the story of Lilliput, where all the people were about six inches tall and quite warlike. During his travels (which Jonathan Swift wrote as political satire), Gulliver visited many countries, including one where the people were giants, as much larger than Gulliver as he was than the Lilliputians.

The first edition of the book was published in 1726. In the second edition, Jonathan Swift included a map. On it he sketched his imaginary countries onto unfamiliar areas of the known world. Brobdingnag, the land of the giants, was placed at the northwest corner of North America, where it appears as a good-sized mass of land with a peninsula hanging from its southern edge.

Fourteen years later, Vitus Bering and Alexei Chirikov sailed from Russia and discovered Alaska, the first non-natives to see and identify the territory. Alaska—on the northwest edge of North America. Alaska—a large landmass with a southern peninsula. Alaska—land of giant animals such as grizzly bears, polar bears, whales, walrus, and moose. There is no way Swift could have known any of this. I discovered the astounding coincidence in *Alaska Off the Beaten Path Guide Book* by Melissa DeVaughn when I researched my 2002 trip.

When I drove to Alaska, I took a one-day ocean cruise from Seward, on the Kenai Peninsula. In addition to acupressure bands and a behind-the-ear patch, I was carrying Bonine, ginger, and peppermint to combat motion sickness. And something must have worked, for I had only a few moments of queasiness as the boat bounced across the waves.

Our captain pointed out a whale ("Watch for a spout on the right") and otters ("Shh, they're sleeping"). And he told us the story of Resurrection Bay.

In 1792, Alexander Baranof's ship was seriously damaged in a storm, with broken masts and leaks in the hull. In vain they limped along the southern shores of Alaska, seeking a deep bay with an accessible shore, a stand of tall straight trees, and shelter from the wind. The crew knew if they weren't able to make repairs soon, they would never see their homes again.

On Easter they entered a bay that had all they needed. Baranof told his men that, just as God had raised Jesus on Easter morning to give mankind the opportunity to be saved, so He had provided this bay to give them the chance to return to their families. And he wrote the name "Resurrection Bay" on his map.

Suddenly the rather boring bit of ocean teemed with connections and interest.

Chapter 15: Your RV Toolbox
Think Locally

Happiness in Your Own Backyard

You don't have to go halfway across the continent to have fun.

My mindset often seems to be that distant equals exotic and local means boring. It's my Alaska trip I talk about, my Maine trip I plan in detail, my visit to a friend in British Columbia I cherish.

But weekend or one-week jaunts can be just as much fun, are definitely less expensive, and don't take me away from my students and home duties.

Estes Park is only an hour's drive from my house in Boulder, Colorado. I can leave after school on Friday and be there well before sunset.

Saturday starts with a pancake breakfast in Elk Meadow Campground. Then I may drive Trail Ridge Road in Rocky Mountain National Park, investigate a few trails, enjoy the wildflowers and lakes, and perhaps doze under the pines.

Sunday provides time for a worship service at the campground and another couple of hours in the park before I head back home, refreshed, with rolls of film to develop.

Breckenridge, only a couple of hours from home, provides a different view of the mountains. Astounding vistas, cool mountain streams to dabble my toes in—this also is utterly delightful.

I am always amazed at people who never see nearby sites unless they have out-of-town company. At home in Boulder, I enjoy visiting the Celestial Seasonings® Tea Factory (a small friend calls it "Special Sneezings"). My local mountains and trails are as invigorating and inspiring as any in the country.

Looking for easy destinations for a one-week trip in Colorado, I have the Colorado National Monument near Fruita, Glenwood's natural springs, Mesa Verde, Four Corners (where you can stand in four states at once) … I could go on and on. And then there are the adjoining states, too.

Oh, you're probably thinking, *she lives in beautiful Colorado! If she lived where I live, she wouldn't be satisfied with local sights.*

Every area has hidden (or not-so-hidden) treasures of scenery, museums, and historical interest. Weekend jaunts keep the RV wheels moving and seem to whet the appetite for more full-length trips.

A friend challenged me on this statement, so I did a little research. *Where have I been that's really boring?* I thought. *And, what's interesting to do there?*

Okay, I went to Cornell College in Mount Vernon, Iowa. I have spent the intervening decades describing the town as "a spot of intellectual brightness totally surrounded by corn fields." Is there anything fun in Mount Vernon—not the surrounding countryside, not nearby cities … *in* Mount Vernon?

Well, there's a skateboarding park. Several city parks including one with hiking and bike trails, fishing, a dock, and a pretty little lake. Victorian-style houses. What the Web site describes as a "quaint business district." And, of course, the college, which has a gorgeous, stone chapel. In autumn, the town is overhung with the hues of maples and oaks. Sounds to me like a place that would take more than one day to see completely.

How about another example? Well, I frequently drive through Coeur d'Alene, Idaho. As I recall, they have a few fast food restaurants and gas stations. I stop, fill tank and tummy, walk the dog, and drive on to more interesting places. Then I went to their Web site, where I learned that in the county are "eighty-seven parks and campgrounds, forty-seven hiking trails, fishing, swimming, hiking, golfing, horseback riding, softball, tennis, amusement parks," water parks, family fun centers, and five state parks. I think I'll add it to my next Northwest itinerary.

The focus of my family's summer vacation was a six-week trip covering one quarter of the country. This is what we planned and talked about. Nonetheless, every year when I was a child, we drove into the Missouri Ozarks, no more than two hours away, one weekend each autumn to enjoy the fall color. Each spring we went back, to see the redbud and dogwood in glorious bloom. Those trips became an important tradition for our family.

So don't just focus on major, continent-spanning vacations. Plan some local trips, and lower your stress. Decide how far you can drive Friday after work, if your rig is packed and ready to go. Mark that radius on a local map (you can use a pencil and string if you don't have a compass, or just eyeball it). Then investigate: call or e-mail the Chamber of Commerce or Tourist Bureau in each county in your circle; check tour guides; talk with friends. And you'll be a treasure-hunter, finding hidden gems around every corner … an explorer seeking adventure in unknown terrain … a connoisseur of the under-appreciated. Oh, and you'll have a great time, too!

Tools for Planning Local Trips

- How far can you go after work/school on Friday?
- Mark that distance and draw a circle on your map.
- Check with the Chamber of Commerce, friends, the Internet—what's to do in that area?
- Do it!

Travel Is Pretty Simple
Six TIPS for Having Fun When You're Stranded Somewhere

In bad weather, if you have car trouble, when you're hopelessly lost,

1. Go to the library.
2. Get tourist info fliers at the campground, motel/hotel office.
3. Check at the Visitor Center, Chamber of Commerce.
4. Ask at the grocery store, gas station, etc.
5. Look in the phone book.
6. Ask questions:

    What is there to do around here?
    What's this town/area known for?
    What should I see while I'm here?

Chapter 16: Side Trip to Big Basin Prairie Preserve, Kansas June 2000

Alabaster Cities

Boring? Only if I want it to be.

"Ha!" I said suddenly, putting my finger on a spot at the bottom of the Kansas map and startling the cat, who leapt up and knocked over my stack of tour guides.

I was looking for a more interesting way across Kansas than my usual route on the interstate. Big Basin Prairie Preserve gave me a goal, and I headed south from I-70 the next morning toward Dodge City on US 283. There I got a handout at the Visitor Center, which gave directions to the Preserve as well as information on the Basin itself: "For 1.4 miles, U.S. Highway 283 traverses the floor of Big Basin, which most likely resulted from salts dissolving several hundred feet below the earth's surface and causing subsidence of the earth above it. This site preserves mixed grass prairie that is rich with wildflowers during spring."

O-kay. I stopped at the Big Basin historical marker. Then, just a few yards down the road, I found the entrance to the park itself. It was a gravel road, one lane, going off into the lone prairie. I pinned my hopes on a line in the flier about a parking area and pressed on, trying not to think of how hard it would be to get the RV out of this place if there were no turn-around. One-and-a-half miles later I found the parking area, where I had lunch.

It was sunny and hot, and I could see buffalo a long way off, grazing on the thick prairie grass. I took a few pictures and found my way out again, taking the Gypsum Hills Scenic Byway east across the bottom of Kansas.

The gypsum hills were beautiful. Wondering what gypsum is, I looked it up: "one of the more common minerals in sedimentary environments. It is a major rock-forming mineral that produces massive beds, usually from precipitation out of highly saline waters, sometimes known as alabaster."

Hm ... alabaster ... as in, "Thine alabaster cities gleam, undimmed by human tears" ("America the Beautiful" by Katharine Lee Bates).

I realized that I had spent an entire day seeing two bits of grassy scenery and fighting the wind along the roads. This back-road travel is slow, I thought, but pleasant and pretty. And God made it all! A little research, some willingness to branch out—what fun I'd had!

Chapter 17: Trip Commentary
Emily's Loop of Utah, June 2004

Best-Laid Plans

Emily built a great itinerary, but none of us knew
what those dark patches on the beach actually were.

"But I *live* in Colorado!" Emily complained. "Why would I want to vacation here?"

Her mother and I glanced at each other. Planning our trips had been simple when Emily was a child. As a teen, however, she had a strong bent toward doing things her own way.

"Why can't we go to California?" she demanded. "I'd like to swim in the ocean."

"We only have about eight days," Diane reminded her with a motherly look. "Go through the AAA guide and see what looks good, okay?"

"Well …," she accepted the TourBook reluctantly. "It's got Utah in it. Can we go there?"

"Sure. Just mark what you like, so we can plan."

Three days later Emily called me.

"I've worked it all out!" she said excitedly. "See, first we go to Vernal, Utah and do dinosaurs. You'll like that, right?"

"Sounds good," I answered.

"Then on the next day we go up to Flaming Gorge," she went on. "We can swim and ride horses, and Mom can sit by the river. Then there's a train ride in Heber. And then we'll go to Salt Lake City. Mom's got friends to visit there, and there's this real cool amusement park. Wait, Elsi! They have a *train*! You'd enjoy that!"

"Well, yeah," I admitted, reluctantly accepting Lagoon Amusement Park.

"And then we take a scenic byway, for Mom, to Moab. The church youth group went there, and it's cool! And maybe Glenwood on the way home. How's it sound?"

Actually, it sounded good. So we followed Emily's itinerary. Diane and I added the Great Salt Lake, based on fond childhood memories. It had been a strange experience, being in water with such a high salt content that my buoyancy was out of control. I remembered how much fun it was to lie on top of the water, and laughing because my swimming suit was stiff with salt the next day.

Our trip was during an extended drought, so we had to walk a long way to reach the water. We could see a few other tourists scattered across the sand and in the lake itself. There were also dark patches, which I assumed were wet sand, shallow spots, or seaweed of some sort. We kept walking.

"Oh, gross! What's that?" Emily asked.

We had reached the first of the darker places on the sand. It was flies, no bigger than a pinhead, stacked knee deep. I waved my walking stick at them to drive them away. This made them fly up, so they were now less compact but shoulder deep.

"Hold your breath, and come on," Diane told her daughter as we waded into the things.

"The Visitor Center mentioned brine flies, but I wasn't thinking of anything like this," I muttered after we were through them.

We eyed the next dark spot with concern. Sure enough, more brine flies. They didn't sting, and they didn't bite. They just flew, quietly, and walked on our skin. I don't think we actually felt them on us, but we thought we did.

"We'll be free of them when we get into the water," I said encouragingly, and we forged on.

The darker areas in the lake were also brine flies.

Emily stopped, making unhappy noises and flapping at the flies with her hands. Diane and I stubbornly continued. We had planned to swim in the Great Salt Lake, and we were going to do it!

Brine flies lick salt. Once we were wet with salt water, they clung thickly to every millimeter of skin, no doubt licking happily. It made my skin crawl.

We waded back out of the lake and almost ran up the beach to the shower area.

"That was really horrible!"

It was indeed. The next morning, reading in Isaiah, I called to Diane, "I know where those flies came from! Listen to this: 'The LORD will bring on you, on your people, and on your father's house such days as have never come since the day that Ephraim separated from Judah, the king of Assyria. In that day the LORD will whistle for the fly that is in the remotest part of the rivers of Egypt and for the bee that is in the land of Assyria.' That's in Isaiah 7:17 and 18."

Emily shuddered. "Yeah, it sure felt like one of those biblical plagues!"

Her mother and I agreed. Nonetheless, the following summer we were all laughing about the experience. And Emily keeps making suggestions for our next trip, "but not where there's brine flies, okay?"

Chapter 18: Your RV Toolbox
Where Should I Camp?

Orphans of the Highway

Don't worry; there's sure to be a campground nearby.

*Then drivedrivedrive, until supper-time, then half an
hour past ... then an hour past ... then another hour and
... but why go into the morbid details? We ate supper at
8:00. And in an abandoned gas station, of all places! We
are poor lonely orphans of the road.*

(my family trip log, 7/1/61)

We were orphans of the highway several times each trip when I was a girl—sleeping in roadside parks, on residential streets, or in parking lots.

About half the states no longer allow overnight stays in their roadside rest areas, though some larger chain stores now welcome campers. I assume, rather cynically, that they hope visitors will spend money when they wake up. I have friends who regularly stay in Wal-Mart lots, but I feel much safer in a campground, thank you.

So, how do you find a good campground? Start by deciding what the purpose of your stay is: Do you just need a safe place to sleep and have breakfast? Do you want to relax by swimming while you're there or check e-mail? Or is the camping experience part of your trip, so that you want scenery, ranger talks, or access to tours?

Amenities

What amenities must you have? I always want electricity, because sleep apnea requires my sleeping with a CPAP machine each night. I need regular e-mail access, because I edit papers for several college students. I don't need sewer and water connections every night, however.

I don't dry camp (called boondocking by RVers) often, because of my CPAP machine. But in the Great Smoky Mountains National Park I decided to try my inverter, which turns battery power into "real" power. I camped at Elkmont Campground, which has no hookups but provides a gorgeous river. There was a constant sound of running water from the river and creeks—so loud I thought there were fans running in the nearby public bathrooms. My inverter worked beautifully, and I learned that one quilt and a beagle are not enough to fend off the cold of 3 AM in the mountains.

When I travel with my friend Diane and her two children, a swimming pool is as essential as electricity. The kids are also thrilled with miniature golf courses, banana bikes for rent, and arcade games.

Some campgrounds, such as the West Yellowstone (Montana) KOA, have a handyman on site. Most have friendly and competent managers who are glad to be helpful.

So, what do *you* need at a campground? Scenery, laundry, propane, sewer dump, modem, pool, TV, game room, meals, electricity, water, cable, a dog run, handyman, church service, tour pickup, showers, store, playground … the possibilities are endless, and only you know what is essential—and that may vary from night to night.

Once you know what your priorities are, how do you choose a specific campground? There are a variety of area and national guides available—KOA, Good Sam, AAA, SKPs, and so forth, all of which are covered in Appendix B.

My father felt strongly about camping in a natural setting. "I would never stay at one of *those* places," he would snort as we drove by a chain campground. But the chains and clubs do offer consistent pricing and quality. I know what I'm getting when I stop at KOA or a facility listed in *Trailer Life*. Looking at the ratings in other guides gives good information, but I've learned to read the guides with care and to ask questions when I make my reservation.

When I traveled to South Carolina for my nephew's college graduation, I chose the campground closest to the university. It was clean, with friendly managers and campers. But "self-contained rigs only" turned out to mean it had no bathrooms, no showers, no laundry. I discovered this too late for my water heater to get the water up to bathing temperature, and ended up clean but shivering at the ceremony that evening.

Stopping in Wyoming for a Dennis Jernigan worship service, I stayed at the only local campground. It was clean and well kept, with managers who attended the service with me. Sunday morning, however, when I got to the showers, I was faced with a locked door.

"Oh, it's much too early in the season for us to turn the water on," the manager told me with a chuckle. I went to church unwashed that morning. I had checked to make sure the campground was open, but hadn't thought to ask about temperature-related issues such as freezing water pipes.

Of course, no amount of careful planning will avoid all problems. At a campground in Watson Lake, Yukon, Canada, I watched a 5th-wheeler back in next to me. The owner then extended his slideout. I *was* able to get my door open most of the way, and there was even about an inch of clearance. Then in the morning, I found a neighboring camper had parked his vehicle across the front of my space, effectively blocking me in. Never had I seen such crowded conditions—worse than a parking lot or truck stop. But the only amenity I cared about there was electricity; I was focused on getting to Alaska.

Reservations

Making reservations in advance gives you a chance to ask pertinent questions, but it ties you to a schedule, also. In fact, you don't need to reserve a campsite ahead of time unless it's a holiday or there's a special event in the area. Or, of course, if you want to stay in one of the national parks—though even there you can find campgrounds on a first-come-first-served basis (I recommend arriving early in the morning; ask if pets are allowed).

If you want to, you can start looking for a campground when you get tired, watching for signs along the highway. There's no guarantee of what you will get that way, but it's not always a bad experience.

One summer I drove to Sheridan, Wyoming, where I discovered it was the closing weekend of their rodeo. "No space available," the clerk at the KOA told me. She had no idea where I might look, either.

As I was about to leave, the owner came in, looked at my rig (and, possibly, took pity on my being a single, limping, old lady), and suggested a semi-site near the basketball court. He even rode his bike over in the killing heat to help me back in.

In my trip log that evening, I wrote, "And here I am, with the power pole on the wrong side, snuggled up to the dumpster and basketball court, and very happy to be here! The RV is beginning to cool off (I got here a couple of hours ago), which is nice. Even Dolphin won't go under the chair; he is on the table where it is somewhat cool. Praise the Lord!"

In Alaska with two friends, I phoned the Williwaw Forest Service Campground near Portage for a reservation.

"Reservations must be made three days in advance," an unhelpful man told me curtly.

We had tour plans the next morning, so we thought hopeful thoughts and drove on. There was a sign at the entrance: CAMPGROUND FULL. In desperation I drove in anyway, planning to ask for suggestions. The campground host (obviously not the person I had spoken with the night before) looked through the windshield as we talked, seeing my friend in the passenger seat with the dog in her lap, and her elderly mother on the sofa with the cat.

"Are you ladies alone?" he asked.

"Yes, we're having a wonderful time!" I told him.

"I have a site for you," he said. "I keep number one saved with a lawnchair, just in case someone really needs it."

"God saved that site for us," my friend said.

In the campground

What do I do in a campground? Sleep, write, check e-mail, and do the week's laundry, primarily. I write in my trip log; then I read the tour guides and get out appropriate maps and information for the next day's drive. I do that frequently, but always either before bed or after breakfast, so the information's in my head when I get on the road.

Some campgrounds provide barbeque dinners, pancake breakfasts, or ice cream socials. Others host special programs, with speakers, slide shows, or videos about area attractions. You can get this information by phoning ahead, but I enjoy driving in and seeing what's available. I count on a pancake breakfast on summer weekends (I carry sugar-free syrup and have only one small pancake, but it's a great treat.)

At the Great Falls, Montana, KOA I heard a talk about artist Charles Russell, who was from the area. And I stayed to hear a couple of singers playing bluegrass on their banjos and taking requests. When I said I was driving to Alaska, they sang "North to Alaska!" Later, they did "Sloop John B" for me and "Amazing Grace," though they weren't familiar with "Little Brown Church in the Vale."

If you tend to retrace the same route, you get to know your favorite campgrounds. In 1958, my family visited Salt Lake City. The trip log reads, in part,

> *Short drive to Salt Lake City, where we found 4-star National Trailer Park, an enchanting spot, all neat and businesslike. Priced according to what luxuries you choose—all concrete, like we had, or a strip of grass, or a strip of grass and a patio. Each space included neatly concealed sewer, water, and electrical hook-ups, and one small tree.*

Eight years later, in 1966,

> *We drove to Salt Lake City, where we found our old stomping ground, the National Trailer and Sleep-in-Car Park. We had a spot with a slender strip of grass and a tree. They charge by the tree.*

In 2004, I stopped at a KOA in Salt Lake City. Memories were stirred, and I spoke at length with the manager. My trip log says, "I asked in the office last night, and again in the morning. And this *was* the National Trailer Park! It opened in 1953. What fun to find the place. And, look at those trees!"

Tools for Finding a Campground

- Campground guides:
    - o   AAA TourBooks and Campground Guides
    - o   KOA Campground Directory
    - o   *Trailer Life* from the Good Sam Club
    - o   SKPs
- Google "campground" and the state or nearest city
- Watch for signs along the highway

Travel Is Pretty Simple
Four TIPS for Campground Activities

1. Take advantage of campground amenities
Use the pool. Check out the game room. Are there bikes or miniature golf? An ice cream social, breakfast or dinner, movie night or special speakers?

2. Walk around, and keep your eyes open!
Make a list of out-of-state license plates. Play an alphabet game, looking for things that start with A, then B, and so forth. Count the pets, and types of pets; I met a caged rabbit at a KOA; my beagle was thrilled! Notice the different things people put in their yards: statues, plants, lights. Notice the scenery, the natural plants, changes in the sky.

3. Take care of routine busy-work.
Do the laundry. Clean and organize the RV. Wash the windows. Dump your holding tanks, and top off your fresh water.

4. Take some personal space.
Check your email. Read a book. Watch a movie. Take a nap. Read through tourist fliers (available in the campground office). Update your trip log. Write postcards.

Chapter 19: Historical Perspective
Bathroom stories

Potty Mouth

Just for fun—almost a history of campground bathrooms …

About two in the morning, when I wake up needing to use the bathroom, I take my handy bathroom for granted. You think I'd know better, but I seldom think about what a blessing it is to have facilities in my RV.

When my parents and I started trailering in the 1950s, we used campground toilets and showers. As a patent lawyer, however, my father searched out the newest and best in technology and conveniences. In our day, that was a Traveling Jon®, a set of folding legs with a toilet seat on them and a plastic bag clipped underneath. What luxury not to have to go outside in the rain or at night!

Of course, there were some drawbacks, as my parents' trip log shows:

8/6/56, Mon.
to Eureka Springs, Ark.
Travel Jon bag broke under Daddy—dire emergency! Very hot—120° in sun. Near lake, but no johns.

Each time we pulled into a campground, as soon as the trailer was leveled and unhitched in our site, I took the teakettle and the dog and headed out. Soon I was back, having done my important jobs.

"Here's water, Mommy. The bathrooms are clean, and there's even a bench by the showers! There's poison ivy under the trees, so I didn't let Poppy walk there. She saw a bunny! Can I play on the playground till supper?"

Reading the family trip logs, I notice we were perhaps overly aware of campground bathrooms:

8/9/58, Thursday
Gallup, New Mex.
Big desert centipede in ladies' john!
8/29/58
Arrived at Glacier to get the last trailer site in Apgar campground—a beautiful little wooded pull-in, and the johns were perfectly gorgeous.

6/21/61, Wed.

We finally stopped in Gambrill State Park, with real flush toilets, women's stand up ones.

7/1/63

Then we drove-drove-drove until late and stopped in a Nebraska rest area, which was amazing! The john building was gorgeous and new, with hot water and soap and paper towels. We're used to box toilets at best, with signs saying "NO CAMPING!"

Showers of blessing?

I treasure my fully equipped rig, but I generally use the campground showers. This is because I'm lazy. Dolphin's litter box lives in my shower stall, and moving it is a nuisance. I don't want my gray water tank to fill up fast, either. And my water heater does a slow job of getting water to a comfortable temperature.

When I was a child, we had no choice but to use campground showers. That was generally a positive experience ...

8/18/58, Sat. (dull day)

Hot—between 90 and 105°. Stopped in a lovely trailer court in San Bernardino. Hot water—tile showers—divine!

7/9/61, Sat.

We headed for Jacques Cartier State Park on the St. Lawrence. It turned out to be a joy. A beautiful park, nice place to camp, and hot water and showers! Just like downtown!

Generally I don't mention showering in my trip logs. The pay showers I used in Canada are an exception. Essentials for showering there are clean clothes, towels, washcloth, shampoo, rinse, soap, and several loonies. Loonies are Canada's $2 coins, and I got five whole minutes of water for each one. I quickly shifted to Mariner Scout mode: get wet, and turn the water off. Use soap and shampoo. Ready? Turn the water back on, and see how fast you can rinse.

I shower either very early in the morning (before the rush) or just after supper (before the swimming crowd comes in). I had been waiting a few minutes one evening when I heard the water turned off in the shower stall. I was utterly taken aback when the shower-er stepped into the public part of the restroom to dry off and dress.

Telling the story to a campground acquaintance later, I laughed when she responded, "Praise the Lord for eyelids, so we don't have to look!"

A few years ago I was traveling with my friend Diane and her middle-school daughter. We walked together through the dusk to the shower house. Three stalls, three people, no waiting—perfect! Each of us stepped into a changing area, stripped, and pulled back the shower curtain.

Which is when we discovered there were no walls between the showers. Emily was intrigued by Diane's and my rather giggly reminscences of junior high showers after PE.

I have become accustomed, in restaurants as well as campgrounds, to self-flushing toilets and self-starting water in the sinks. In Cypress Hills Inter-Provincial Park (Alberta and Saskatchewan), though, I had a self-starting shower, with an electric eye at about stomach level. Ah, the wonders of modern technology!

The olden days had some things going for them, though:

8/15/58, Fri.

Luscious 3-star trailer park in Reno, where we played canasta while the rain pattered on the roof, and then took nice showers, Elsi & Mommy in adjoining showers, harmonizing on "Desert Silv'ry Blue" and passing the shampoo under the partition.

Chapter 20: Trip Commentary
Estes Park, September 2001

Camping in the Rain

Don't let a little rain ... well, even a lot of rain ... spoil your fun!

Estes Park, Colorado, is about an hour from my house, not much longer than to my dentist (and a lot more fun). Perfect for a weekend getaway.

We shoved baskets of clothing and bags of food haphazardly into cabinets on Friday after school. My friend Diane and I had papers to grade; Emily had a social studies project and some spelling homework; Ryan was carrying his algebra book. We were going to combine work with pleasure over the weekend.

It started raining about sunset, when we were halfway there. Luckily there was little traffic. I straddled the centerline to avoid the branches roiling down the side of the road. The shoulder was a river, with gushing muddy water overflowing onto the road and bringing gravel and small (two-fist size and less) rocks with it. I was mournfully singing, "The Lord said to Noah, There's gonna be a floody, floody," as we splashed into our campground.

While Diane and the kids attempted to make order out of the chaos inside, I sloshed around outside in the dark, connecting the electricity. Then I stuck my head inside, asking, "Does the microwave show we have power? Good! Will some-one hand me Lady's leash?"

I scooped my reluctant dog out and dropped her in a shallow spot. She cast me a look of total betrayal as I closed the door in her face.

"Go outdoors," I commanded. "Go outdoors—and quickly, please!"

I followed her with the flashlight as she ducked under the RV to take care of her business. Then I carried her back inside and dried her firmly with the beagle towel stashed by the door. She ran to my bed to finish the drying process on the quilt, and I shed my soggy shoes and socks before hanging my raincoat in the shower.

I woke up in the morning humming something, as is my custom. Then I noticed what I was singing, and had to stifle my giggles so I didn't wake my guests:

Step into the water! Wade out a little bit deeper!
Wet your feet in the water of His love!
Step into the water! Wade out a little bit deeper!
Come join angels singing praises to the Lamb above!

When Emily and I took Lady out in the morning, the air was crisp, the mud was solidifying, and the sky glowed with a blue that appeared freshly washed and waxed.

"Mom, come see the holes in the road!" Emily called when we returned and I was drying Lady's feet.

"It's quite something," I agreed. "In some places there are eroded spots four or five feet deep! I don't know how we got in here without falling into one of them!"

We spent the morning playing miniature golf on beautifully landscaped courses (both Meadow and Mountain), riding bumper boats, and eating hotdogs at Cascade Creek Mini-Golf.

In the afternoon we drove into Rocky Mountain National Park, where it rained again as we walked around Bear Lake. As we slogged soggily along the last leg of the trail, we passed a wet family, wrapped in raincoats and with umbrellas. The father said cheerfully, "Lovely, liquid Colorado sunshine!" No one else in the group smiled.

"The pine smells so fresh," Diane commented, just as Ryan stopped in the middle of the trail.

"Look!" He pointed across the little lake. "A double rainbow!"

Again we sang of Noah's flood and its glorious ending, then headed back to the RV for supper. Emily did not seem happy while we were eating, however.

"What's wrong?" I asked.

"Mom promised we could make s'mores," she grumbled, "but it's wet!"

"The wood's dry," I said, "because it's in a storage compartment in the RV's basement."

"What about homework?" Diane asked.

"I did most of it when we drove up last night," Emily said quickly. "And I can finish tomorrow morning early. Can we, Mom?"

"Let's find some roasting sticks!"

Ryan chose to do algebra while it was quiet, and Dolphin stayed to help him.

"Elsi, your cat is sitting on my book!" Ryan complained as we left.

With Lady's assistance, Emily, Diane, and I built a fire in a handy tent-site fire circle and made s'mores, with creative variations. Can you build a s'more, then balance it on the stick and cook it whole? No. How about poking the stick through the piece of chocolate? Nope. Wrapping marshmallow around the chocolate before roasting? Uh-uh. Building a box with the crackers, held together with sticky marshmallow, and filling it with chocolate? Sorry!

We carefully doused our fire, though it would have taken a blowtorch to set anything alight after all that rain, and went peacefully to bed.

In the middle of the night, I was awakened by a persistent beeping. I pulled myself out of sleep, found my glasses, and investigated. It was the carbon monoxide detector. Ryan got up to help; so did Dolphin. Lady woke Diane and Emily, and there we all were, at 2 in the morning, listening to the soft *beep! beep! beep!*

I opened all the windows before digging out the folder of manuals and reading about the carbon monoxide detector.

"It's not a real problem," I announced a few minutes later. "This is the low-battery sound, not the emergency one."

"Does that mean we can close the windows?" Emily was shivering.

Ryan closed windows while I attempted to get the detector off the ceiling so we could shush it. Ryan and his pocketknife succeeded eventually, but we couldn't figure out what to do next. After a while, in sleepy desperation, we evicted the beeping monstrosity to the picnic table and went back to bed. I got the campground handyman to replace the batteries for me the next day.

Elk Meadow Campground's traditional Sunday morning pancake breakfast offered two delicious pancakes and two fairly good sausages, plus OJ and coffee. Back in the RV, Emily responsibly did her homework, Ryan took a shower, and Diane and I chatted while marking papers.

Later, in the lodge, a group gathered for a worship service. A volunteer from Texas enthusiastically played the piano, and we sang gospel choruses. The service was led by the RV park electrician, Tom, who asked Ryan (as a recently returned summer missionary) to open us with prayer. There followed a skit about the Lord's Prayer, some discussion of prayer, and a few more choruses. A lovely way to start a mountain Sunday.

Driving back down the mountain after lunch, with the sun reflecting off the roof of the car in front of me, Diane and I talked about our students.

"I think this weekend's left me ready to deal with those kindergarteners," Diane said.

And Emily suddenly interjected, "Wasn't the storm *fun?!*"

Chapter 21: Your RV Toolbox
Getting Oriented in Space

Spatially Challenged

All about not getting lost, and what to do when you are.

My name is Elsi, and I'm spatially challenged.

"Hi, Elsi!"

Maybe, as a friend suggests, it's due to my having grown up in a town where all the main roads were parallel to the Mississippi River. Or perhaps it's because I had no depth perception until I got glasses at the age of nine.

All I know is that I'm never quite sure where I am in space. Will my car fit between the curb and that bus? Am I all the way at the front of the parking space? If I turned left to get here, do I turn left or right to get home again?

Living in Boulder, Colorado, it's easy for me to forget that I have no innate sense of direction. If you tell me to go two blocks north, I'll just look around until I spot the mountains, twist my body a bit so that my left shoulder is towards them, and—ah ha!—I know where north is.

I manage. I don't do jigsaw puzzles. I may miss some parking places. But I get by.

Then I bought an RV and headed out across the continent. I felt a bit like poor Charlie on "The MTA" (a popular Kingston Trio song written in 1948): "Did he ever return? No, he never returned, and his fate is still unlearned!"

I have a compass in my RV, but I have been known to miss my turn while trying to work out which way, if I'm currently going south-southeast, will send me southwest. Oh, well.

Sunrise, sunset

One summer, happily driving along US 101, the Pacific Coast Highway—which parallels the coast through Washington, Oregon, and California—I spotted a sign through the fog: "BEACH ACCESS."

I turned off the highway and prepared to play: change to water shoes, grab the camera, put the dog on her leash … *let's go!*

And we did have a wonderful time. Lady galloped in and out of the waves while I waded. I took pictures of her rolling in the sand and chasing seagulls. As the fog thinned, I got shots of the ocean, disappearing into the distance.

Eventually Lady and I headed back to the RV, where I washed six sandy feet, put on my dry shoes, and settled in the driver's seat to continue my trip. Except … I couldn't remember which way I had turned when I left the highway. So I didn't know which way to turn in order to continue in the right direction.

As I tried to decide if I should just guess and take the chance of driving for an hour or more the wrong way, a car pulled into the turnout behind me, and I hopped out.

"Can you help me?" I said. "I was driving south on 101, and turned out here to play on the beach. Now I can't remember whether I turned left or right off the highway, so I don't know which way to turn to head south."

With an embarrassed laugh, I added, "I do fairly well in Denver, because the mountains are always on the west. But here … I'm really confused!"

"Ma'am," the driver responded with commendable restraint, "this is the Pacific Ocean. It's always on the west."

See? Spatially challenged for sure. I bought a compass at the next opportunity.

Several friends have suggested I get a GPS (Global Positioning System) for my rig. I have a couple of concerns about that. For one thing, I'm not good at technological gadgets. I'm smart enough to learn the system, but I'm not sure it would be worth the trouble. Which brings up another issue. Perhaps I could use it to help me plan a route. But, once I'm lost, who is going to power up the laptop and key in the information while I'm driving around? The cat enjoys typing, but he does not follow directions. And the dog is interested only in love and food.

Planning and following a route

So I plan my route thoroughly, highlighting my state map in bright colors. I mark directions in my itinerary: "W I-90 to Mead WA—exit 281, US 395N to US 2: Cat Tales Zoological Park (feed lion); 1 hr; T-Su 10-6."

But even with that amount of detail, I got lost trying to find Cat Tales. Finally I asked at a grocery store, where I was helpfully told, "Go on down that road out there a-ways. You'll know the park because they have a giraffe out front." As it turned out, the building with the giraffe was a taxidermist, but I did eventually get to the Cat Tales Zoo, where I got to hand-feed raw chicken necks to a liger (lion-tiger cross).

KOA does a great job of giving specific directions to their campgrounds. AAA tends to focus on street addresses, which is not always helpful. MapQuest gives corner-by-corner directions, but they're not always accurate, as they warn you on their Web site. Sometimes Web sites give good information, and I've been known to phone places and ask for more specific details. The "real people" on the other end of the phone line are always helpful: "It's just past the old gas station that burned down, and then you'll see a hamburger stand before the turn." That's my kind of directions.

I type my directions in short, easy-to-read lines. I will have to refer to those directions while I'm driving, so they need to be clear enough that I can get each step with one glance.

I print the itinerary a day to a page, unless I'm staying several days in one place (such as a national park or with friends). The page for the current day is on the RV console, within easy reach, along with any maps covering the day's trip. I review each time I stop (bathroom, snack, dog walking), so I stay on top of things.

Leaping to Conclusions

In *The Phantom Tollbooth* (Norton Juster), a boy and his friends are traveling in a toy automobile. In the midst of a conversation, they find themselves off the highway and on a strange island. Eventually they realize they have been making assumptions and have, therefore, leapt to the Island of Conclusions.

When I find myself in a strange place, or the wrong place, or an unknown place, I try not to leap to conclusions. The first step is consciously not panicking. I remind myself that the world won't end if I miss the train ride or whatever.

Then I attempt to decide whether I'm really lost or just disoriented. If I think I am going in the wrong direction, I stop and ask for help. This is not always easy in the rural West; you can drive a long time before finding anyone to ask or spotting something on your direction list. I just keep going, assuming there will be something fun to do or see somewhere, even if I miss my intended destination.

I've also been known to pull over, have a snack, take a walk, and regroup mentally before getting back on the highway. As I drive on, I will probably be singing one of these songs, apparently written for the circumstances: "Lead Me Gently Home," "Lead On, O King Eternal," "Precious Lord, Take My Hand," "Guide Me O Thou Great Jehovah," or "Day by Day My Savior Leads Me." Because if He's leading me, I'm not really lost, am I?

I always do make it back home, and I generally have a great time doing it, too!

Tools for Dealing with Feeling Lost

- Don't get lost:
    - o   Plan your route.
    - o   Get directions in advance.
    - o   Mark your maps.
- Don't panic if you do get lost:
    - o   Have a compass and/or GPS system for reference.
    - o   Have a cell phone to call for help.
    - o   Don't fret or let being lost ruin your fun; calm down and know you'll come through all right.
    - o   Look for ways to enjoy yourself, wherever you wind up.

Chapter 22: Trip Commentary
Searching for a Train

Lost? No, I Found It!

I thought I was lost, but I kept driving till I found the right place.

The Sumpter Valley Narrow Gauge Railroad sounded like a great little train—of course, I like all tourist trains. My map wasn't too helpful in plotting a course to the station, which apparently was in an unmarked, tan spot southwest of town. The eastern part of the Oregon map has a lot of unmarked tan spots, I noticed. I had taken the precaution of getting directions in the campground to supplement the AAA and train guide ones, but….

I drove through beautiful woods, admiring the flowers and hills, enjoying the bright sky. And looking in vain for signs advertising the train. County fair signs, yes, but nothing about the train.

I drove on, and on, and on. I checked my compass occasionally, but the road twisted so often the pointer seemed to spin randomly. I tried to phone the station, but found (no surprise) I was in one of the dead areas with no cell access. Panicking wouldn't help, I told myself firmly, so I just kept driving. After all, as Isaac Watts wrote in "I Sing the Mighty Power of God," "And everywhere that man can be, Thou, God, art present there!"

Eventually I found my way through town to highway 7, which I took to McEwan, Oregon. McEwan almost doesn't exist—it's not really a town at all (as far as I could tell), just the railroad station. Lady and I walked up to the station to make sure I could get a ticket—I wasn't sure but that everyone at the county fair would be wanting to ride the train. Apparently all the everyones were wanting to see the Shrine parade, however.

There were very few of us on the train, which was nice. I asked the conductor which was the better side for seeing scenery, and he suggested I ride on the left going out, and in the caboose cupola coming back. What a treat—I was so glad I had persevered.

Just as I entered Idaho later that afternoon, there were two bales of hay on a bridge in the traffic lanes, with cars swerving all over to avoid them. I stopped at the Welcome Center not a mile down the road to tell them.

They told me, "Oh, yes, we reported it, and the police responded."

I said, "No, they didn't do anything about it."

"Well, we saw them go by."

"That's nice, but they didn't *do* anything!"

So the Welcome Center lady called again, and I drove on.

I stopped a bit later to get something to eat and phone a KOA for reservations. And again to go to the bathroom and grab some supper. That one was awkward; I chose an exit with no corresponding entrance, though there wasn't a sign indicating this. So I drove through the tiny town, seeking the interstate, reminding myself that God knew where I was, so I wasn't *really* lost.

Back on the highway, I eventually landed in Twin Falls, Idaho, at a nice KOA. They have breakfast in the morning, a good modem connection, and pleasantly treed sites. After laundry and e-mail, we went walking in the evening, both cat and dog enjoying the smells and people around us. And Twin Falls is on the map, which was a comfort.

<u>Chapter 23: Side Trip to Battle Ground, Indiana</u>
<u>October 6, 2004; May 9, 2006; October 9, 2006</u>

Lost? Yes, But Look What I Found!

I just followed the road, and discovered wolves!

My intention was to take I-80 around Chicago and into Indiana, where I would find a welcome center and get an Indiana map and some directions. I'd forgotten that I-80 becomes a toll road at Chicago, but that was okay. Trouble was, they had major road construction. Speeds ranged from full stop to perhaps 10 mph for about half an hour, then rocketed to 20 and even 30 mph as I moved into Indiana. All this with lanes going in odd directions and merging with little notice, and heavy, rush-hour-type traffic. I succeeded admirably at staying in my lane, following traffic, and coping, in spite of this being my first trip with my new (and longer) RV.

When my lane suddenly exited, however, I saw no choice but to go with it. I drove south for quite a while before I spotted a Visitor Center sign and got re-oriented. I was near Wolf Park and it sounded intriguing, so I immediately added it to my itinerary. Once there, I asked about petting a wolf, which had been mentioned in both the AAA guide and the flier from the Visitor Center.

"All you have to do is adopt one," the attendant told me.

I filled out the paperwork and handed over my credit card. She processed it and said cheerfully, "Now, just call us two weeks before you want to come in, and we'll set up a visit with your wolf."

"You know," I said as gently as I could, "I live in Colorado. I am in Indiana now. I cannot give you two weeks' notice for this visit. *Please*, may I pet a wolf?"

"Well … that depends," she said thoughtfully. "Do you know which wolf you want to adopt?"

"Absolutely! I know exactly what wolf I want!"

Her face showed concern.

"I want to adopt a wolf who is available to be petted *now*."

So, laughing, she signed me up for Deneb, who was elderly with arthritic hips, just like me. We had a lovely time. I rubbed her ears and tummy, and kissed her nose, and stroked her thick fur. My dog and cat sniffed me thoroughly when I returned to the RV.

A year passed, during which time I bought a pumpkin stuffed with treats for Deneb's Thanksgiving. Then she died of old age, and I was assigned another wolf.

The next spring I headed for Indiana, eager to meet Wotan, just a year old. I made an appointment in advance this time, participated in the training program, and went out to meet my wolfling.

They wouldn't let me go in the wolf enclosure, because of my cane—it might be a chew toy, and I wasn't fully stable without it, especially under the loving leaps of 150 pounds of wolf. So the trainer brought Wotan out on a chain leash to my bench.

But Wotan had no interest in his Aunt Elsi at all. He did what my students would have done; he ran up and down the road by the fence, saying to the other wolves, "Ha ha ha! See me? I'm out here, and you're not! Ha ha ha!"

The trainer kept guiding him by me, and several times I got my fingertips on his fur as he passed. But he had more interesting things to do than make friendly to an old lady from Colorado.

Finally he rolled on his back in protest, and the trainer said, "I think he's done" and returned him to the enclosure.

I sat on my bench, thinking, *You're an adult. You will not whine and complain. You will not mention how much money you spent and how many miles you drove to do this. You will be a big girl and a good sport!*

But my trainer caught the next wolf who came along, an older adolescent named Renki. And Renki *liked* his Aunt Elsi! Renki almost climbed into my lap to be patted! We had a delightful time.

And when I left, I called, "When Wolf Park writes to suggest I buy a pumpkin or watermelon stuffed with treats for my wolf, Renki is getting it. Tough on you, Wotan!"

My students loved hearing the story and seeing pictures of Renki and Wotan. Third-grade Zach kept repeating, "Tough on you, Wotan! You said, 'Tough on you, Wotan!'"

Well, what do you know, teachers are human, too.

Postscript: On my fall-color trip that fall, I visited Wotan and Renki again. Wotan was happy to see me this time, and I was thrilled to be allowed in the large enclosure with the pack—six adolescent wolves, leaping around, leaving muddy paw prints on my shirt, licking my face, and asking to be patted. Zach was pleased to know I'd given Wotan another chance.

And I was pleased, too. I was raised that the proper response to being lost was to become angry; Mother once wrote in our trip log,

6/23/61

Off we rolled to Hershey, with smoke pouring from Daddy's ears as we kept getting lost. How Daddy hates to get lost—he mutters what must be dreadful swear words about the inefficiency of the highway marking system, and gets more and more bitter.

My ability to roll with the confusion, figure out where I was, and find interesting things to do there made me feel competent ... and helped me be less concerned the next time I was lost.

The Great Salt Lake was covered with brine flies; they are the darker patches on the water. They didn't bite, but they walked all over us, licking salt—it made our skin crawl, as you can tell from the look on poor Emily's face.

I rode the Kit Carson County Carousel in Burlington, CO, with pleasure.

Dolphin got his walk before my carousel ride.
He is sure he is a saber-toothed tiger,
stalking dinosaurs in the wild jungle.

What a fantastic experience,
to pat and play with Wotan, my adopted wolf,
at Wolf Park in Battle Ground, Indiana.
photo courtesy of Monty Sloan
wolfphotography.com

→ *PART 3: WHAT ABOUT SAFETY?*

Chapter 24: Your RV Toolbox
Is It Safe to Travel Alone?

No Need to Panic

Of course, I'm safe!
I've never been harmed in a decade of solo travel.

"There's no way I can be at conferences till ten and safely drive an hour and a half home in the dark," I told my principal. "And if I do make it home, I'll never be awake enough to drive back in the morning. Can I drive my RV to school and camp in the parking lot overnight?"

So, with the agreement of the principal and the building engineer, that's what I did. My class took a mini-field trip to the parking lot to see my RV and meet the dog and cat. And that night, after conferences were over, I walked the dog, crawled into my bed, and went to sleep.

I'm not sure what time it was—certainly well after midnight—when I came abruptly awake. There were lights glaring through my windows, someone was pounding on the door, and Lady was baying wildly. A voice was yelling, "Open up! Police!" I found my glasses and went to the door.

I glanced out the window to verify the presence of a police car, grabbed Lady's collar firmly, and opened the door. Immediately a flashlight beam was in my face. I spared a thought of gratitude that my pajamas are presentable as I put my hand up to block the light.

"This isn't a campground," the officer said, moving the beam slightly to the left.

"Yes, sir, I know." I was fumbling for an explanation. "See, I'm a teacher here, and we had conferences …"

Lady nosed forward, and the policeman automatically reached out to rub her ears. As I continued to talk, the cat pushed around my other side, and the officer set down his light to reach out to her, too. (Had I been a criminal, this would have been my chance.)

"Nobody told us you'd be here," he told me. "We're responsible for keeping the school grounds safe."

"Yes, sir. I'm glad you're being careful. You can call the District security office if you want to; they know I'm here."

"That's all right, ma'am. Sorry to bother you."

With a last pat, he and his partner drove away. I relocked the door, had a soothing snack, and went back to bed.

I wasn't frightened till it was all over. Then my mind started churning: *What if they hadn't been policemen? What if the cat had gotten out? What if . . .* This was not helpful, of course.

Taking basic precautions—no different from those I take when I'm at home—was key here, as it usually is when something comes up. I did check that it was a police car; I did have a hand on the cat . . . no problem!

Frightened but okay

I've been frightened a few other times, too. In Alaska, another driver started patting Lady while traffic was stopped for construction. When we got going again, he followed me, stopping at each gas station I went to, inviting me to visit him at his home in Anchorage. I finally took his card and thanked him. He left, and I tore up the card. Whew! (And if he hadn't? Again, it's no different from when I'm home—threaten to call the police; call the police; ask for help in a store or gas station.)

In 1966, as a college student traveling with my parents, I was in real danger but didn't know it. I naïvely wrote in the family trip log, "Suddenly, in the midst of a barren desert, the new (i.e., retread) tire gave up its tread. Plop. So Daddy and I changed it with great rapidity and no trouble (except a helpful man who impressed Mother as being a rapist)."

What were the facts? Mother had taken the dog and walked away from the road. Daddy had jacked up the trailer and loosened the lug nuts, then burrowed under the bed in the trailer, trying to reach the spare tire (which was behind all the stuff we planned to use). I was sitting on the side of the road, happily removing lug nuts, when a car stopped.

"Need any help?" the driver asked.

"No, thanks," I said, continuing to twirl the spanner.

"I'd be glad to give you a hand," he persisted.

"I'm doing just fine."

He walked over to me. "That's a dirty job. Let me help you."

"No, thanks," I repeated.

From the trailer, my father called, "What did you say, Elsi?"

"I was talking to a man who's offering to help us out," I answered.

And when I looked up, the man was disappearing down the road.

I was nineteen when this happened, and totally naïve. Now I think I would have figured out what the "helpful" man had in mind. And then? Pretend I had a companion; grab for a cell phone; step into the highway and pray a car would come along.

Staying in touch

Of course, I wouldn't want to be on the road for six or eight weeks without anyone's knowing where I am. Giving someone a detailed plan does not ensure that, even if you stick to it precisely. I learned this when I was eleven.

If my father's itinerary said we would drive west on Highway 47 and turn south on Highway 172 at noon, there was no point in reading the signs advertising a new zoo just off the highway. It was not on our list, and we would not go there. We had to stick to the plan.

My father's secretary had our itinerary, plus a description of our rig: a gray-and-cream station wagon pulling a matching trailer with a large, red dragon painted on the back. So, when my grandfather died, the secretary contacted the Oregon highway patrol. With a trailer that obvious and definite information as to where we were, they could easily find us.

Or so we thought. We made a scheduled mail pickup a week later and found out we had missed the funeral.

I have a detailed itinerary, and I leave it with friends before I leave, including campground phone numbers. But I have no qualms about leaving out planned stops, adding new ones, or totally changing my plans when I spot something intriguing, such as spending an afternoon on the *Lady Washington*, a sailing ship off the Washington coast. If something happens that I need to know about, my friends can reach me via e-mail, which I check almost every night.

I carry an Emergency Contact card in my wallet all the time. It has information about my hypoglycemia and medication sensitivities, plus phone numbers for several friends, a description of my RV with its license plate number, and insurance information. A copy of that card is in my beltpack, the front pocket of my backpack, on the console, and on the counter by the sink in the RV.

Backing alone

"One of my earliest memories is standing at the back of a campsite, yelling *Left* or *Stop!* as Daddy backed the trailer in," I told Lady. "So why won't you sit back there and bark—once for left, twice for right, a bay for stop—how hard can this be?"

She wagged her tail agreeably, yawned, and lay down for a nap. Oh, well.

As a new RVer, I always asked for a pull-through space in campgrounds. If I had to back into a space, I requested help from someone there. Or, if I really had to back in alone, I would get out and check how far I was from the tree, the water connection, the picnic table. Backing into a 30-foot space, I could walk around the RV verifying distances up to 20 times.

After a couple of years, a friend told me, "Before you drive that thing to Alaska, I'm going to teach you to back up."

Freedom! Phil showed me how to adjust the spot mirrors so I could see my back corners. He coached me until I knew what I should be seeing in each mirror, so I could re-adjust them myself. And he took me to a school parking lot, empty on the weekend, for backing practice. With buckets and buoys for markers, plus patience, Phil helped me practice until I could back smoothly into a space.

My Alaska photo album and trip log have several comments along the lines of, "And I backed into this all by myself! Thanks, Phil!"

That was really all I needed to be independent. Dealing with electricity and water connections was easy—I'm touched but amused at the sweet managers at some campgrounds who offer to take care of that for me. Would I be out if I couldn't do this?

Try again another day

I generally know about how far I will get each day. Sometimes, however, I pull over early. In fact, that's often the solution to difficult driving situations.

If I am falling asleep as I drive, I will find a roadside rest area and sleep for half an hour. One summer, with temperatures in the 90s, I went to a KOA and asked for "an hour's worth of electricity, so I can plug in my air conditioner and take a nap." The kind proprietor charged me as a tent; I got my nap and drove home safely.

Sometimes I stop early because my arthritic hip is too painful to continue. Other times a traffic problem or weather causes a premature end to the day.

In crosswinds, the RV feels like a mobile billboard. If, with my thumbs locked around the steering wheel and my elbows braced on the armrests, I am still being blown out of my lane, I find a place to stop.

Once, walking Lady in a rest area while I waited for the wind to die down, I overheard truckers talking about "last night's tornado." No wonder the wind felt so strong!

Another time when I was astounded at the force of the wind, I got out at a rest area—and discovered the "wet road" was actually ice-covered. So much for my vow to *never* drive on icy roads. I did drive on, but very slowly.

Lady and Dolphin love the early stops. They provide opportunity for an extra snack, additional beagle-patters, and (if the cat is very lucky) birds to watch through the window.

And I check my e-mail, put in a CD, update my trip log, and curl up with a good book and a cup of sugar-free cocoa, safe and happy for the evening.

Tools for Being Safe

- Have a communication plan for family and friends.
- Make ID cards with emergency contact info; keep them visible in the rig.
- Hide money and credit cards in an unlikely place (under litter box, in a first aid kit).
- Sign up for an emergency protection plan for your vehicle(s).
- Use the same common sense that you use at home:
    o   Don't be too friendly with strangers.
    o   Lock your door.
    o   Be wary, especially if you're not in a campground.
    o   Obey your internal "vibes" or concerns.
- Nonetheless, have fun!

Travel Is Pretty Simple
Five TIPS for Safe Weather Driving

In rain, snow, sleet, ice, wind, …

1. If it's dangerous (tornado, too-strong wind, heavy fog), get off the road:
    a.   Out of your rig and into shelter
    b.   Under an overpass
    c.   In a rest area
    d.   On the shoulder
2. Slow down (just as you would in a car).
3. Be aware: in high wind, semis and overpasses will block the wind briefly, but then you drive back into it.
4. Stay in your lane.
5. Pray.

Travel Is Pretty Simple
Six TIPS for What to Have with You if You're Hurt and Alone

1. Your health insurance card
2. Contact information for your emergency trip insurance—
   a. Care for your pets
   b. Make arrangements for children or dependents
   c. Cancel reservations later in the trip
   d. Return or store your RV
3. Phone numbers or email for your doctor, dentist, and so forth
4. Phone number or email for your lawyer
5. Phone numbers for friends who might help in an emergency
6. Phone number for your insurance agent
7. Extra credit card and debit card
8. Copies of prescriptions and spare glasses

Chapter 25: Side Trip to Brown County State Park, Indiana
October 2004

Don't Drive Anywhere You Can't Get Out of Again

Be sure to check for an exit before driving into a parking lot.

"Aspen gold is nice," I say each fall, "but it's so monochrome!"

I grew up in the Midwest, where the hills are splotched with all colors in autumn. I cannot get too excited over Colorado's golden aspen.

On my first fall-leaf trip in my new, 30-foot RV, I exulted in the rich colors across the Missouri Ozark region. Then I drove into Indiana, aiming for Brown County. In Brown County is the Brown County State Park, which claims some of the best color in the Midwest.

The leaves were gorgeous, vibrant, with branches arching over the road. When I spotted a sign for a scenic overlook, I turned off the main road. To my surprise, there was no through road, no exit. I would have to turn around. *(Ominous music, please.)*

I parked along one side of the lot and climbed the hill to the stone overlook. The thesaurus only begins to offer enough color words to describe the trees: gold, deep rich yellow, red, crimson, scarlet, burgundy, cherry, brown, chocolate, russet, orange, ginger. Perhaps an artist could name every tone and hue; all I could do was admire, take pictures, and enjoy a sign: *What a terrible time of year to be an evergreen tree!*

Then I returned to my rig. I walked around it, wishing I could just pick the thing up and set it down facing the other way. At last I decided I could make a 90 degree turn into a parking space and back out, pointed in the other direction. I located a large, empty space to start in, and settled in the driver's seat.

A car zipped into the lot and pulled into "my" space.

I waited. Another space opened up, and just as quickly filled.

At last I got out again and waited for a friendly looking woman to walk by. I explained my situation. "So, would you keep cars out of that spot till I'm in it please? And then guide me in backing out?"

She was glad to. I swung into the space while she stopped traffic. Then I opened my windows and tried to watch and listen while she directed me, "A little more to the right. More right! Stop! Back straight! No, I mean, left! Pull forward a little! Good! Now back left! More! A little more! *STOP!*"

I thanked her and returned to the main road. At each scenic turnout after that, I came to a full stop in the road, peering up the side road to be sure I could get out again.

Yes, if I'd been a bit more careful before whipping into that scenic turnout, I would have seen even more beauty. That's all right. It may have been a terrible time of year to be an evergreen, but it was the perfect time to be a traveler.

Chapter 26: Your RV Toolbox
Be Prepared to Deal with Hazards and Problems

Oh, Dear! Now What?

You can handle problems on the road; I guarantee it.

I am convinced that the highway department has hacked into my McIntosh computer. What other explanation is there for the fact that my itineraries always lead me to road construction?

"Okay, guys, she's going to Utah on I-70 in July. Find an excuse to dig up the road!"

That's what happens. I have no doubt.

Of course, I'm kidding. It was my father who took bad road conditions as a personal challenge.

8/19/58, Tues.

A "drivedrivedrive" day. Decided to pass up Rocky Mountain Park and keep going. Tackled the Berthoud Pass—right at the first we had to pull out and pass a long line of cars held up by a truck, 'cause if we'd stopped on that incline, we'd never have gotten going again. Against the yellow line, too, and many irate drivers honking furiously.

You're going to meet problems along the road. There's really no avoiding that. But there's no point in seeing them as either attack or challenge. Find a way to deal with them, and move on.

For example, I was driving happily along South Dakota county roads one June, headed for De Smet, a Laura Ingalls Wilder site. I came over a slight rise and was startled to see a house in the middle of the road. There were several cars behind the house, and I joined the group. Eventually the movers came to a dirt road into the cornfield and pulled as far over as they could.

The cars in front of me went around, with their left wheels partway down the slope. I sat there, considering. At twelve feet high, I wasn't sure how far I could safely slant before falling over. And the overhang of the house roof meant I couldn't stay right against the house. Slowly, painfully, I started to inch by. I noticed I was hunching my shoulders together in a futile effort to make my RV narrower.

People behind me were honking. Eventually one of the house movers came around the side to find out what the hold-up was. His eyes widened when he saw me, and he guided me with hand motions until I was safely past.

I waved my thanks, expelled a deep sigh of relief, and drove on, humming "We're off to see the Wizard!"

Funny, in retrospect

My travel issues have usually been minor. Once I left my gas cap at a gas station and stopped at an auto supply store for a replacement.

"I don't know the size," I admitted after explaining what I needed.

"No problem," the clerk said cheerfully. "Just bring in the old one, and we'll match it."

Uh-huh. I explained, gently, that the whole point of my problem was that I didn't have the cap. He laughed, apologized, and came out to look at my vehicle so he could identify what I needed. I could have kept driving without one, but I didn't like the thought of what might be falling into my gas tank.

At one gas station, I had to phone the credit card company because of a hold on my card. They thought it had been stolen when major activity showed up out of my normal area. Now I call before I leave, telling them where I'm going and warning them it may take three or more swipes of the card to fill my tank.

My rig stopped without notice one Sunday evening on the Kansas interstate. I coasted to the shoulder and phoned my Good Sam Emergency Road service.

"We'll send a tow truck right out," the woman told me. "What is your ZIP code?"

I thought irritably, *I can give you the milepost number; how am I expected to know ZIP codes as I drive?*

I explained this. The Good Sam representative must have used a map to find me by the milepost, because she sent a tow truck at once. The tow truck took me into Topeka, depositing me in the parking lot of a Ford dealership. When they opened up in the morning, there I was.

"Looks like a bad fuel pump," they told me after due consideration. "It'll take most of the day to get a new one here."

So the dog and I moved into the waiting room, where helpful employees kept turning the TV on for me, and I kept turning it off. Half an hour later, the service representative came in.

"You're all ready to go! You were just out of gas."

"But I checked the gauge!"

"So did we. A piece broke off the emissions control stuff in the fuel tank, and the broken piece blocked the float that monitors the level of gas in the tank."

Two times I've lost all power in my rig, which is how I learned about Ground Fault Interrupters and the emergency power switch Winnebago sweetly put right where I kick it as I go out the door. Minor, but a nuisance. Though I keep kicking the thing, I now know how to solve the problem.

Power issues are not uncommon, but they're not apt to ruin more than an evening:

7/20/58, Sun.
leave Valley City, ND
Found Sacagawea's statue, and saw fascinating Mandan Indian village. Then drove and drove (during one stretch, Mother did not kill a flock of sheep, but did break off trailer brake handle!) through dull South Dakota—so much prairie, and nothing to see. Nice park—free, too, and a swim in the Missouri river. But when night fell, so did disaster—something wrong with twelve-volt lights. Too late and dark to fix, so Elsi read by flashlight until we all went to bed for lack of illumination.

The hose came off once when I was dumping my tanks, but it was only gray water (thank God!).

I got trapped in a gas station without enough room to turn to leave. A few customers yelled at me, but some kind people helped me back and fill until I could get out.

Each of those incidents was upsetting at the time, but I dealt with them. No vacation was ruined or even seriously marred. God has protected me against serious problems, but He has also helped me develop a good attitude—which is helpful sometimes …

In Yukon Territory, I watched the family in the site next to mine spend the evening re-adjusting their satellite dish and grumbling about getting poor reception.

When I was walking the dog that night, I stopped to chat with them.

"Are you headed to Alaska, or on your way home?" I asked.

"Well, we *were* going up there," the man told me, "but we're not going now."

"Oh, I'm sorry! Why not?"

The man gestured around the campground.

"Too many dirty rigs!"

So what?

Afraid your rig will get dirty? Get out a hose. And avoid tailgating on dirt and gravel roads.

There are too many trains and carousels to ride, too many museums and historic sites to visit, too many scenic pullouts ... just flat-out too much beauty and excitement across our continent to let a flat tire, dirty rigs, traffic hazards, or even gas prices interfere with my enjoyment—or yours.

Tools for Dealing with Those Inevitable Problems

- Know where your fuses, circuit breakers, and power switches are.
- Inform your credit card companies that you'll be traveling.
- Practice looking on the bright side.
- Ask for help when there's a problem.

Travel Is Pretty Simple
Seven TIPS for Staying Safe and Happy on Drivedrivedrive Days

To keep yourself safe:
1. Stop and take a power nap if you get sleepy.
2. Take short walks to stretch your legs and restore circulation when you stop.
3. Listen to books on tape or CD.
4. Listen to and sing along with music on CD or radio; driver's choice.
5. Have snacks available within reach (in a cooler by your seat, for example), so you don't have to stop to eat.

To amuse your passengers:
1. Create a contest for who pays for mid-afternoon ice cream (most blue cars, most different license plates, most different animals spotted, ...).
2. Passengers can play board/card games (magnetic chess, checkers, etc.).
3. Play car games.
4. Passengers can do crafts (sticker books, weaving, knitting, etc.).
5. Someone can read aloud (stories, tour guides books).

Travel Is Pretty Simple
Ten TIPS on What You Need in Emergency Road Service (ERS)

I use Good Sam, but there are many other ERS programs out there. These are the basics to look for when you're choosing one to meet your needs.

1. 24/7 emergency dispatch service across the United States and Canada
2. Program that is focused on the needs of a large RV
3. Protection for all your family's vehicles, including bikes and boat trailers
4. Flat-tire service—repair, replace, tow
5. Locksmith if you're locked out
6. Jump starts or free tow
7. Fuel delivery if you're out of gas
8. Travel delay assistance: help with emergency travel expenses
9. Emergency medical referral service
10. Easy access to ERS personnel and information, by phone or on the Web

Chapter 27: Your RV Toolbox
But I'm Disabled; Can I Do This?

I Get By—with a Little Help from My Friends

Easy? Not always.
Fortunately I find friends everywhere.

I pulled off at the first rest area I saw.

"Wow, that really hurts!" I said to the dog, who was scratching at the door. "Give me a minute, then I'll take you out."

Wincing, I climbed out of the driver's seat. Walking didn't relieve the pain in my leg and hip. Neither did --*ouch!*-- mild stretching exercises.

Bending to clip leash to collar was painful. I hobbled to the nearest patch of grass, ignoring Lady's eagerness to sniff every bush and greet every traveler.

Back in the RV—the steps were misery—I gulped some ibuprofen and lay down, wondering what was wrong. My arthritic hip could be plenty uncomfortable, but this went clear to the ball of my foot.

Back on the highway, I discovered that cruise control allowed me to change speed with my thumb, so I could rest my right leg a bit. Using my left foot on the brake pedal helped, too. Creative arrangement of small pillows took some of the pressure off my hip. I crawled into a Tom Clancy novel on tape and tried to ignore the pain.

I took more ibu at bedtime. About one in the morning I gave up and pulled out my emergency medical kit. Bee stings … sunburn … I'm sure put it in here after that root canal, just in case … somewhere … there! The Vicodin® eventually helped me sleep. In the morning, though, barely half an hour's driving triggered the pain again. I was still in Utah, and there had been an avalanche on I-70 in Colorado, with a winding detour that precluded use of cruise control. It was going to be a long trip home.

Mobility problems

Discomfort, on the road or elsewhere, was not new to me. My arthritic hip flares up without notice—a bit like the cat, actually. Stairs are hard for me. So is any distance walking, or steep inclines, or uneven terrain. The first step in coping with this was to get the right RV and equip it properly. I switched to a Class A RV to gain easier access to the driver's seat, and I had double handholds installed by the door so I could get in and out more readily.

The ADA (Americans with Disabilities Act) has seen to it that elevators and ramps are available in museums and other public buildings. Many stores and museums have electric carts available. I zip through the aisles, checking out sales, piling my purchases in the basket at the front. Of course, some of the carts have an annoying safety feature: they beep loudly in reverse. I recall being camped in Yukon Territory, on my way to Alaska. Someone pulled in next to me about 2 AM, with a reverse beeper. The dog, cat, and I came fully awake; so, I'm sure, did most of the other campers in the area. The cart's beeper isn't that bad, and I smile wryly and try to ignore it.

At home I carry a handicapped parking placard. My first one was temporary, good for 90 days.

"Wonderful!" I told the Department of Motor Vehicles man. "So you're guaranteeing I'll be healed in three months?"

Not everyone appreciates my odd sense of humor.

Now I have a permanent placard—good for three years. Three years is permanent? Goodness!

If I towed a car, I could use my parking permit. But my bad hip is one of the main reasons I don't tow a car; I just don't see myself hitching and unhitching.

In the Downtown St. Louis RV park, I watched a woman back her rig in, unhitch her tow vehicle, and connect her power and water. Then she tossed her wheelchair into the car, called her children to climb in the back, and drove away. I was impressed, but not ready to step up to that challenge.

My mother had multiple sclerosis and used a wheelchair for many years. Daddy and I learned a lot through that experience. For example, wheelchairs don't fit down the aisle of an airplane. Two beagles are strong enough to pull a wheelchair, but they won't cooperate well enough to do it effectively. A person in a wheelchair is handy for holding packages and coats. And (my father's discovery), do not attempt to push a wheelchair across the beach.

When an electric cart isn't available and I'm with friends, I use a wheelchair. On a school field trip to the Denver Museum of Science and Technology, I checked out a wheelchair and allowed the children to push me. They thought this a great treat and vied for the privilege of "taking care of Mrs. Dodge." One girl parked me outside the restroom and told a classmate, "Watch her till I get back!"

In DisneyWorld I rented a wheelchair, and Diane's kids pushed me around. It was very helpful, and not just for me. When Diane's mother got tired, I walked, using the wheelchair for balance, and she rode. And when Emily succumbed to the heat, she was able to ride, too.

I'm astounded at how relatively inaccessible Canada is. My mother had multiple sclerosis before the ADA passed, and I've had some experience with shoving her wheelchair through crowded aisles in stores and wrestling it over rocks and dips on woodland trails. But I've grown accustomed to the assumption that all places are open to everyone.

Then I drove to Canada. What a beautiful country, and such nice people! I did find two handicap-accessible tourist sites, both nationally run. The Storyeum in Vancouver (British Columbia) has wheelchairs for checkout and an elevator; the Frank Slide Interpretive Centre in Frank (Alberta) has ramps. But even the visitor information buildings often have steps, and one campground I stopped at actually had steps to the showers. I love driving through Canada, and I'll go back—but I'm glad I can still walk and climb stairs when I have to.

Other disabilities—the RV actually is a help

I have central sleep apnea and use a machine to help me breathe at night. Oddly enough, I might never been diagnosed without the RV. My friend Diane said to me, "You know, I never actually sleep in the RV. Either you're snoring so loud I can't sleep, or you're not breathing and I'm afraid you're dead!"

I failed the screening questionnaire for sleep apnea, because it requires you to have a bed partner: *Do you kick in your sleep? Are you a restless sleeper? Do you jerk or turn over a lot?* My dog refused to answer these questions. But Diane's comment got me tested, and now I actually get rest at night.

I do, however, require electricity to power my machine. So I got an inverter, which takes battery electricity and turns it into "real" electricity. I've only used it once, but it's nice to know I can continue to sleep if the power goes out.

I have blood sugar problems and require a specialized diet. Here again, the RV really is an asset: I have my own kitchen, with everything I need. I can stop and eat on my own schedule; I carry insulated lunch bags and blue ice in my backpack when I'm being a tourist. If my blood sugar is too low and I need to rest (or if I run out of energy), I can sleep in my own bed. Even in midsummer, I can park in the shade, open my windows, and get a half-hour nap before it gets too hot to bear. And I can stop and camp whenever I want or need to.

I think RVs were created for people with anxiety attacks. That's why I named my first rig the *Travelin' Tortoise*, because I had my home with me, a safe place to retreat to if I needed it. Unfamiliar places, strangers, crowds … these could send me into a panic attack at any time.

I visited Henry Ford's Greenfield Village, near Detroit, paid for my ticket (a pricey $25) and headed for the train station. After riding the train, I looked at my map … and panicked. Too many people, too many choices, I didn't know what to do. So I went back to the parking lot, had a snack, and took a nap. When I was calm again, I returned to the park.

My first writers conference (Colorado Christian Writers Conference, in Estes Park, Colorado) was possible only because I took my RV. There was no way I could have stayed in the lodge, with or without a roommate. Knowing I had a way to retreat if I needed to, secure that my dog was nearby, I was able to attend the sessions profitably.

Cheerful empathy

There are some advantages to all this. I have a small collection of adorable canes, one with a moose head for the handle, another with a turtle. If I'm going to limp around, I'm going to do it with flare! I have an aspen walking stick I use for sand or water, places I don't want to risk my personality canes.

A much older woman, inching along with a cane, stared at me as I passed her in a store lobby.

"You sure are moving fast!" she commented.

"That's because you're using a cane … and I'm using a moose!" I responded with a grin.

I hate being in pain, feeling helpless. Everything I do, I analyze: Is this worth the pain it will cause? In Glacier National Park, the tour bus driver was passionate about Sunrift Gorge. He parked just off the road and sent us up the trail, telling us we just couldn't miss this. I wasn't the only one limping as we came back down the steep path, but the view was well worth the discomfort.

My doctor willingly renews my prescription for pain medication, knowing I will take it only when necessary and only for sleep. If I am well-rested, I can better bear whatever aches and pains the day brings me.

I use a backpack so my hands are free to help me maneuver. I rest when I need to. I carry supplemental health coverage, so I can see a doctor if I need to while on the road. I ask other tourists about accessibility before starting up a trail: How steep is it? What's it like up there?

Staring up a steep, winding path in Zion, I asked a tourist coming down, "Does it level out up there?"

"Nope," he said cheerfully, "but it's a real easy walk! And it's kinda pretty, actually!"

He strode on; I turned back. Not going to risk that one, thanks.

I am often reminded of Jacob, who wrestled with a man (or God, or an angel). "When the man saw that he could not overpower him, he touched the socket of

Jacob's hip so that his hip was wrenched" (Genesis 32:25). My hip is wrenched, and I have a new empathy for people with mobility difficulties, people in chronic pain.

Meanwhile, back at the ranch

At the beginning of this chapter, I was in Utah, facing a long, painful trip home. By the time I got home through the avalanche detour, I was in so much pain I couldn't sit for more than a few minutes. No writing, no scrapbooking. My shoulders ached, because I was lying on my back, holding a book up so I could read.

The doctors finally decided I had an inflamed disk, complicated by arthritis. A steroid shot, exercise, and physical therapy helped a lot. I used a cushion to ease the sitting difficulty.

I was already begnning to plan my spring trip. My itinerary was based on pain-management, allowing for the possibility of driving a couple of hours, then popping a pill and sleeping a couple of hours. Few definite stops, plenty of flexibility, don't give in to this problem.

This was a good plan, but I didn't need it. I did all sorts of fun things on that trip, because I was able to drive almost painfree. *Wow!* I thought. *This is unbelievable!*

I visited my wolf at Wolf Park, stopped to see several friends, and went to my nephew's wedding. I went to Kennesaw, Georgia and saw the *General*, the real locomotive from Disney's *Great Locomotive Chase*.

So don't let your disability stop you—it hasn't stopped me. But oh, I can't wait for my new body in heaven! I will dance before His throne with grace and abandon.

Tools for Traveling with a Disability

- Carry whatever aids you need
    - o Cane, wheelchair, scooter
    - o Parking placard (useful to prove need)
- Know your medications
    - o Carry a copy of prescriptions
    - o List medications on Emergency Contact card
- Don't worry about accessibility in the US
    - o Phone ahead in Canada.

Chapter 28: Trip Commentary
Fort Clatsop on Wheels

Roll That Scooter

I didn't need that handicap scooter … did I?

The sun was shining as I drove past the shuttle bus to Fort Clatsop, where Lewis and Clark's Corps of Discovery "wintered over" on the Columbia River in western Oregon.

"I like this system," I said to the dog. Fort Clatsop is one of an increasing number of our state and national parks to use outside parking and frequent bus service in an effort to reduce pollution and traffic congestion.

The next turn was the parking lot, with *handicapped parking* and *NO RV* signs. It was almost half a mile to the RV parking lot. I gave Lady a quick walk, opened the windows, and checked the water dish before heading out, with cane and pack, for the shuttle.

"That was a horribly long walk!" I complained as I limped over to the ranger, twisting and stretching my leg in a futile attempt to relieve the pain in my hip.

"You should have parked in the handicap area," he responded.

"There's not enough room for my RV," I explained.

"Well, why didn't you have a member of your party drop you off?" he asked.

"I've never succeeded in teaching the dog to drive," I laughed.

He looked at me, unsmiling. "You should have made arrangements ahead of time then."

I turned away in disgust.

As I stepped off the bus at the Visitor Center, I realized I could hardly walk. Hobbling to the desk, I said, "I need to whine at somebody!"

I poured out my frustration, not forgetting my anger at the other ranger's dismissive attitude, and ended, "And now I'm too tired and in too much pain to enjoy the site!"

"You're welcome to use our ADA scooter," she offered.

"No, thanks, I'm not that … well, okay, why not?"

"We had an ADA rep show us how to use it," she explained as she wheeled it out. "He toured the entire site. He told us later that his main purpose was to try to roll it on the paths and turns, but he wasn't able to, even at full speed!"

The controls were simple: an on/off switch, levers for forward and reverse, and a speed control, helpfully marked with a turtle at one extreme and a rabbit at the other. I hung my camera around my neck, put my cane and pack in the little basket, and drove out the door.

I started at the fort itself, a replica of the one Lewis and Clark stayed in for 106 interminable days their last winter out—it didn't rain on only twelve of those days, and just half of those twelve had sun. The rooms were tiny but nicely displayed. In one, two costumed guides let me try a quill pen. How the men managed to write those lengthy diaries, not to mention Lewis's reports to Jefferson … unbelievable! I'll take my ballpoint, thank you, or my laptop, any day.

The scooter has major advantages, too. I could go anywhere without pain or stress, and I could get out and walk when I wanted to. I walked in the fort itself, but just parked at the flintlock gun demonstration. Children stared, either curious or jealous. People made room for me when I stopped to look at something; they often do that when I'm just carrying my cane, too.

Of course, sometimes people are completely oblivious. I remember pushing Mother's wheelchair through stores and coming to a knot of shoppers visiting in the middle of the aisle. They glanced at us, then continued their conversation without moving. Sometimes when I'm going up stairs with my cane, clinging to the handrail with my other hand, I have to tell even adults, "I need the handrail so I can get up these stairs, please." And occasionally that is followed by, "So I'm asking you to move over so I can keep going!" But most people are aware, and kind.

I tootled down to the spring, enjoying the forest along the way. I certainly didn't attempt to roll the scooter, but I went at rabbit speed and felt safe. I kept thinking, *It would be agony if I had to walk down this path. And impossible for me to walk back up again! Thank You, Lord!*

I went clear down to the river to admire the dugout canoes. I don't think we would have liked them in Mariner Girl Scouts, but they're impressive.

Reciting Robert Frost's, "The woods are lovely, dark and deep" as I cruised through the forest, I went back to the Visitor Center to tour the museum, thanked the people at the desk, and rode down on the shuttle. Apparently some phone calls had been made, as the ranger below was waiting to push me in a wheelchair back to the RV.

With my hip and leg rested, I was able to walk on the beach later in the afternoon and sleep almost pain-free. Those scooters are a wonderful invention; someday I will want to own one. In the meantime, I will limp along, enjoying the sights.

Chapter 29: Your RV Toolbox
Finding a Church on the Road

Drive-by Church

Finding a place to worship on the highway

"I do want to worship Sunday," I told the Lord before my first RV trip. "But You'll have to make it easy for me, please."

At that time I suffered panic attacks in groups and unfamiliar places. In fact, a major reason for having an RV was to allow me to travel, with a safe haven to retreat to when necessary. So the thought of walking into a strange church was more than scary.

There was a little worship service the first Saturday evening at my KOA. If I didn't find a church to visit Sunday morning, I decided, I'd count that.

But I chose slacks instead of shorts Sunday morning and drove into town. At the first stoplight I glanced left, saw a cross, and made the turn. It was a nondenominational church with plenty of space in their parking lot. A sign said the service would start in ten minutes. Okay—that's about as easy as I could ask.

And it was a good service. The music, prayer, and teaching pulled me into the experience, and I didn't even glance at my watch to see how much longer it would be.

With that as encouragement, I began to conquer my fear and embark on a series of what I refer to as "drive-by" churches. That is, I drive by a church, and if they're having a service in the next 20 minutes or so I stop. I like having structured time each Sunday to worship and learn.

Of course, not every Sunday is as simple as that first time. When I'm traveling state or county roads, I literally drive past churches. On an interstate, however, I have to exit, drive into town, and return to the highway. One Sunday I tried several times before finding a church. Its service was almost an hour away, though, and I could see no place to park 30 feet of rig. Eventually I gave up, singing with a praise and worship CD as I drove on.

At a small church in Rawlins, Wyoming, I was welcomed by over half the adults in the congregation. The worship leader thanked me after the service for singing the tenor counter-part on the old gospel songs. Fun!

Are there alternatives to the drive-by approach? Sure! Many campgrounds offer lists of local churches, available when registering or posted in the laundry room. A biker dude at a gas station in Wyoming gave me careful, corner-by-corner directions to the local Baptist church one Sunday. A campground manager in British Columbia phoned a friend to pick me up for church in the morning.

Church among strangers? Well, we're all part of the "family of God." I've stayed for pancake meals, accepted invitations to lunch, and found Lady lots of lovely beagle-patters in the parking lot.

Looking for a church next Sunday? There's one out there, just waiting for you!

Tools for Finding a Church

- Ask for church suggestions in stores, gas stations, the campground office, and fellow campers
- Check the yellow pages, newspaper, or laundry room for lists of churches
- Keep your eyes open as you drive into town
- Trust the Lord to direct you

Travel Is Pretty Simple
Four TIPS for Traveling with God

1. Remember that He made everything and declared it was good.
   a. The heavens declare the glory of God; the skies proclaim the work of his hands (Psalm 19:1).
   b. The earth is the Lord's, and everything in it, the world, and all who live in it (Ps 24:1).
   c. Psalm 148
2. Carry a concordance or use an Internet one to find references to what you're seeing and doing: http://bible.crosswalk.com/
3. Carry a hymnal or go to an Internet hymnal; use the topical index (especially look under Nature): http://www.cyberhymnal.org/
4. Look also for references to being a stranger or traveler, journey, lost, guide, lead, beauty, creation.

Chapter 30: Side Trip to Yellowstone National Park, Wyoming June 2004

Worship Service with Old Faithful

My Chinese friend and I worshiped at the Old Faithful Inn.

"A picture impress me so much, when Elsi stand in the Sunday worship service, when she sing the hymns, you know, she lift her hands. And this kind of act just make me feel He is reaching His hand. I just feel moved. It's a lovely picture. It's a beautiful picture."

A friend from China and I were visiting Yellowstone National Park. On Sunday we drove to Old Faithful and went to a morning worship service on an outside deck.

Old Faithful went off during the silent prayer. I said, "Even Old Faithful lifts its hands in praise to the Lord!"

"We have our worship service Sunday morning," Angela reported later. "It's very special. Because I come from China, most of the other Christians feel impressed. I can tell that they feel the power God has from their eyes. Because they think, even a Chinese has belief in God, the family is so big, not only focus on Americans. They really hope that God's love is spread to every corner of the world.

"This is first time I feel so proud when I say I'm a Christian and my nationality is China in front of so many people. Those Christians show love to me, and I appreciate that. What I want to say is I'm so blessed, not only to see the natural beauty but also help me feel the love, the blessing I get every day.

"And also the Sunday morning we stand outside, it's the first time I have worship service outside. Old Faithful is really an amazing name, because it makes me realize to be real faithful to God, how to be a real faithful Christian. And actually, several of these American hymns I have sung before in Chinese church. This also reminds me the world is so small. Though the lyrics are a different language, the melody is the same and, more importantly, we are relying on the same God."

I was fascinated by Lassen Volcanic National Park, where a photographer was on-site when the volcano erupted!

I rode the ADA-approved scooter through Fort Clatsop, rocketing down the trails and seeing all the sights.

I'm sure it's a comfort to know Dolphin is available to drive in an emergency.

→ PART 4: LIVING WITH OTHERS

Chapter 31: Your RV Toolbox
Wagon-Training

Parallel Travel

Each with your own RV but traveling together

"Oh, you drove all the way alone? You are so brave! I could never do that!"

I hear this, or some variant of it, at least once a trip.

I don't argue. I don't try to explain that my pets are good company and I stay in touch with friends via e-mail. I just smile and say, "Oh, I enjoy it." And change the subject.

I do enjoy it. I love the freedom solo travel gives me. I love working out my itinerary, choosing my own schedule, stopping when I want to, napping when I need to, and living what my grandmother would have called "a ladylike life of leisure."

Riding the Whitewater Valley tourist train in Connorsville, Indiana, I got into a discussion with some members of an Airstream group about rallies and caravans. They were enthusiastic about the concept, "because you're with other people and get to see things and go places."

"And," a gentleman explained, "you don't have to waste time planning your trip. They take care of all that for you."

One woman told me with genuine excitement, "One of the rallies had 1,500 rigs at it. It was like a small town; we even had our own post office."

That is far from attractive to me. Of course, if it's what you like, that's great—go for it! I think it's wonderful that God made us all different, with a variety of wants, needs, and interests.

Teachers and parents of preschoolers talk about parallel play. This is a developmental stage in which two or more children are participating in the same activity, perhaps several toddlers busily digging in a sandbox, or a group of little boys driving their toy cars around the floor.

Well, the furthest I'm apt to go in the direction of a rally is parallel travel, more commonly known as wagon-training. Back in pioneer times, each family had its own covered wagon. However, it was far too dangerous for a single wagon to go West on its own. Instead, groups would travel together in a wagon train. RVers have borrowed this concept: when two or more families travel together, each in their own rig, we call it wagon-training.

Towing horses

A couple of times I've gone to a friend's mountain cabin. While everyone else slept on sofas and took turns in the bathroom and kitchen, I was independent in the privacy of my RV.

On one of those trips, Bob's jeep blew the engine and transmission. He had brought his horses up in a trailer; now he had no way to get them home. It would take a couple of days and at least $8,000 to repair the car. Bob couldn't leave the horses at the cabin, and the next day was his daughter's first day in first grade.

I offered to tow the horse trailer with my RV. So we headed down the mountain, with another friend driving. We were coming around a curve, hardly out of town, when Phil pulled over suddenly. He had seen an oncoming car miss the curve and fly over the drop-off. Bob and Phil ran back and forced the door open to get the teenaged driver out of the car. She was dazed and frightened, so we took her back to town and helped her contact her father. She told us her flip-flop had gotten jammed under the accelerator.

Several hours later we again left town. As we passed the accident site, Bob pointed out that the car could not be seen from the road. Had we not been there, who knows how long it would have been before she was found?

Oh, and Bob's car?

He told me, "It ended up being a $26 sensor. I think the Lord just needed us in that place where the young lady flew off, at that specific time. I think we might have saved her life. God sometimes works real hard to put us where He needs us."

Family radios

Three times my parallel traveling companions have been a family from church: Paul and Brenda and their children, Reed and Brittany. Paul towed his trailer, and I followed in my RV.

Our first trip, we found we needed communication between the two vehicles. Paul had missed a sign and was headed east at highway speeds. I chased after him, flashing my lights, honking, and driving on the shoulder to catch his attention.

So, we carried "family radios" on our next trips together. A family radio works somewhat like a CB radio, but you can choose your frequency in order to have relatively private conversations. We haven't needed them for emergencies, but we enjoy pointing out interesting sights and having serious discussions about the necessity for an ice cream stop. The radios are useful, too, for passing essential information: "I'm running out of gas" and "Can we make a bathroom stop?"

Our traveling styles were not congruent, but we had so much fun together that we adapted and compromised. I learned to sit around the RV for hours every morning, waiting for them to wake up and eat a full breakfast. They learned to stop for snacks, meals, and dog walks. I cheerfully drove past turnouts I wanted to see; they cheerfully stopped at places they weren't interested in. On our 2004 trip together, we saw two Laura Ingalls Wilder sites (for Brittany and me), visited the Jefferson National Expansion Memorial in St. Louis (Reed and me), and rode one of the Gateway Arch Riverboats on the Mississippi (which we all enjoyed). Then they headed east, and I headed west, spending a week wandering the Missouri Ozarks on my way back to Colorado.

While we were together, we participated in several car games. Our first trip, we limited ourselves to a state license plate contest and a list of animals spotted (does road kill count? Well, …). But for the St. Louis trip I developed a challenge. The people in each vehicle were to spot as many names as they could: names of people, tribes, historical events. At least one of the young people had to be able to explain the significance of the name. The car that had fewer names at the end of the day had to pay for ice cream.

I lost both days.

Little children start with parallel play and grow into genuinely interactive relationships. Similarly, my parallel camping experiences have led me into relationship with others.

Let's see, does that mean my RV is just a big toy? Hey, I won't argue.

Tools for Wagon-Training

- Be sure each person on the trip has at least one best or favorite activity to look forward to
- Discuss variant travel styles and how to compromise
- Have a way to communicate between vehicles
- Have fun and unify the different groups/families with games, ice cream stops, and so forth

Chapter 32: Your RV Toolbox
Friends Who Sleep in Your Rig

Dolphin and Lady Will Gladly Share

How to include non-family members in your trip and rig

It's hard to be a houseguest, adjusting to your host's schedule and sharing a bathroom.

It's even harder when the "house" you're a guest in is 10 by 30 feet, and you sleep in the kitchen. Not to mention sharing your bed with a nocturnal cat who rattles the blinds, complains loudly about private issues, and uses your stomach as a trampoline at three in the morning.

In spite of all this, several intrepid friends have accepted my suggestion, "Let's take a trip together! I'll drive."

I find it's not easy to be a hostess either, especially since I live alone and am, shall we say, somewhat set in my ways. But I keep making the offer anyway, and it's always worth it. My enjoyment can be multiplied when I'm with a friend.

Before we leave, though, a few policies need to be established:

—I have baskets for your clothes and toiletries.

—Don't leave the cabinet doors open unless you want the cat nesting in your stuff.

—You'll need something portable for shower supplies. I have small baskets with handles if you don't have something.

—Bring your own food. There's plenty of room in the fridge, freezer, and kitchen cabinets. I only use the microwave, but we also have a stove and oven. By the way, don't leave kitchen cabinets open, either.

—Nothing goes into the toilet except what comes out of your body and the toilet paper I supply—not tissues, not hair from your comb, not anything.

—Don't let the cat into the bathroom unsupervised. He's got this thing about disemboweling rolls of TP.

—Don't leave anything lying around. It will be lost or damaged, because either it will slide off while we drive, or it will become a kitty toy. Pens, earrings, glasses, false teeth—if you care about them, put them safely away.

—Never open the outside door unless you know where the cat is.

Have you figured out who rules my RV? That's right! His name is Dolphin, and he loves to travel with me.

Fourth of July in Iowa

"My hometown is having its 125th anniversary this summer," my neighbor told me. "My grandfather helped found the town, and I was raised there."

I enjoy being with my neighbor, an intelligent and active 83-year-old. So she made phone calls, I checked the Internet, and we planned a trip to Iowa.

We turned out to be less than perfect traveling companions. She thought my license plate game was stupid, and she didn't like stopping frequently. I wanted to drive the interstate instead of staying on narrow little back roads. But we adapted, had a good trip, and managed to stay friends.

In Mapleton, Iowa, we plugged in at a tiny campground before going into town. We visited the bank, founded by my friend's grandfather, and the museum, with many family pictures. We found her parents' home and put flowers on the family graves at the cemetery.

And we had the delightful experience of a small-town Fourth of July parade. The Shriners were there with their little cars and their dressage-trained horses. Several farmers drove flag-bedecked tractors. We saw veterans tucked into their old uniforms and troops of Girl and Boy Scouts, all marching proudly with our nation's flag. Floats represented the bank, the florist, local restaurants, churches … and I think every business in town. In one car rode the oldest graduates of the high school, 99 and 101 years old. Children scrambled for candy thrown from the floats. It was a time warp to the gentler, more patriotic days of my childhood, experienced only because of my traveling partner.

Alaskan moose

In the summer of 2002, I drove the Alaska-Canada Highway. My friend Diane and her 67-year-old mother flew to Fairbanks and accompanied me to Denali, Anchorage, and the Seward Peninsula. Then they flew home, and I continued my trip.

I wasn't at all sure how Annelle would handle life in the RV, but she was a real trouper. Of course, she sat up late every evening, putting her hair in pin curls, and she kept forgetting where she had stored her things. On the other hand, every night she shared her pillow with my cat, who also ate from Annelle's spoon at meals.

Walking my dog by the little visitor center at Exit Glacier (in Kenai Fjords National Park), on the way to Seward, I spotted a rack of moose antlers chained to a picnic table.

"Diane! Come take my picture! I want to be a moose!"

I handed her my camera and sat on the step, the antlers framing my head.

"Your turn to be a moose!"

Diane posed while I took the picture.

Annelle, every hair in place, wearing a color-coordinated outfit, watched with a smile.

"Now Lady. Don't you want to be a moose-doggy?"

She didn't. But I held her while Diane got the snapshot.

"That was fun!"

I was grinning as I started back to the RV. But Annelle had other plans.

"I want to be a moose, too!"

So we took her picture with the antlers before getting back on the road, laughing and feeling young together.

Three dogs and a cat?

"Our only hope is in learning how much our heavenly Father desires a close and intimate relationship with His children and becoming the children He says we are," says Dennis Jernigan (www.dennisjernigan.com). His testimony explains that his "is a story of hope ... the reason we sing ... the reason we will never stop praising the Lord Jesus Christ."

Dennis's ministry and music have had a powerful effect on my life. When I heard he was presenting a Night of Praise and Worship in Wyoming, only one state away, I made plans to attend.

"I know you like Dennis's songs," I told a friend. "Want to come along and hear him in person?"

"It sounds good," Vicki admitted. "But I don't have anyone to care for my dogs."

"Oh, you can bring them, too."

So that's what we did.

Lady thought it was a great plan. She can always make room for another beagle-patter. Vicki's boxer, Sammie, would have settled down more readily if she had had a lap to cuddle in, but ended up resting her chin on my knee as I drove. Zoë, a pug, shared Vicki's lap with Lady.

But Dolphin, my dominant little cat, was horrified.

What, he demanded, *have you brought into my RV?*

Sammie and Zoë clustered by the baby gate I'd placed across the bedroom doorway, with Dolphin on the other side. *It's a new friend!* they exulted. *Can we play with it?*

Dolphin retreated to my bed, bristling his tail and muttering loudly, *Get those things out of here!*

As the weekend progressed, Dolphin become somewhat used to his new traveling companions, though he never considered them friends. He even ventured into dog territory, making sure he stayed on the counters, well out of reach.

After church Sunday, we headed back home. As we drove quietly down the highway, Vicki was dozing in the passenger seat, with Zoë limp across her lap. Lady and Sammie were companionably sharing the sofa bed. I was singing along with one of Dennis's CDs.

Suddenly Zoë leapt off Vicki's lap and tumbled to the floor, sniffing and pawing. Vicki came fully alert as her dog was launched.

And Dolphin, who apparently had slipped under the seat to goose Zoë, strolled off, tail a-twitch.

So why bother?

It is a nuisance sometimes to have other people (all right, Dolphin, and other animals, too!) taking up our space and changing our habit patterns and schedule. On the other hand, I do find it helpful to have someone actually checking the map, watching for exits, and getting me a snack occasionally. More to the point, though, I enjoy being with my friends, seeing places I otherwise might have missed, and learning to give (and receive) grace and mercy.

Tools for Sharing Your Rig

- Be sure your friendship is strong enough to withstand sharing tight quarters
- Build in ways to get some personal space
- Give everyone some say in the itinerary and timing
- Bring treats and surprises to brighten rain or traffic difficulties (for adults, too)
- Give your friends a packing list and chore assignments

Tool: Chore List

_____ help put awning up, down
_____ help with connections (water, power, sewer)
_____ help prepare and serve meals
_____ help clean up after meals
_____ wash dishes as necessary
_____ put away dishes, meal prep materials
_____ dump the trash
_____ clean table, counter
_____ clean floor (pick up, sweep, use vacuum)
_____ shake, sweep floor mats
_____ sewer dump
_____ walk dog
_____ feed pets
_____ clean litter box
_____ outside walk-around before leaving
_____ inside walk-around before leaving

Chapter 33: Trip Commentary
Yellowstone Through Alien Eyes

Enjoying the Nature

*I saw Yellowstone National Park a whole new way
when I went there with a Chinese friend.*

"Horse?"

I glanced at the field we were driving by. "Yes, those are horses."

The road curved gently. Lady, my beagle, was asleep on the bed, having finally agreed that Angela could have the navigator's seat.

"Buffalo?"

"No, those are cows. Do you have cows and horses in China?" I asked.

"Only on farm. This not farm." Her tone was doubtful. "What that? Small horse?"

Again I took my eyes off the highway.

"Those are antelope, pronghorn antelope."

"Ant-lope?"

"They're like a small deer."

"Deer! I know deer!"

Angela's vocabulary difficulties sometimes tempted me to believe I was conversing with a three-year-old. This was not the case, however.

"I ask my professor can I write about trip for journalism class. I not diffident girl; I ask in front of all class. My classmates like idea. Do you find it very interesting to know how a Chinese see this park?"

Angela, from mainland China, was working for her master's degree in journalism at the University of Colorado-Boulder. Our relationship, which began at a church outreach to international students, started with my helping edit her papers to improve her grammar. Our growing friendship and my desire to expand her knowledge of America led to our being in my RV now, driving through Wyoming on our way to Yellowstone National Park.

The first night out in Wyoming is boring, I think. I generally end up at the Rock Springs KOA, which is fence-to-fence gravel and has clean showers, modem access, and a total lack of scenery. It's just a stopping point along the way to places of interest.

Angela saw it differently.

"This is my first time since last August, when I came to Boulder, I leave Colorado. It's so meaningful to me—Wyoming! We went to registration. Everything totally new for me. We need to plug into electricity. We fill water. We take shower. All those things."

Moose and marshmallows

We pulled into Grand Teton National Park, took pictures at the sign, and dropped by the Visitor Center. On our way to Colter Bay Campground, where I had reservations, we saw cars parked on both sides of the road and a crowd in the distance. I found a wide spot for the RV, and we headed across the field.

"Someone saw a moose!" a woman told us excitedly.

But, look as we might, there was nothing to be seen but other excited tourists, several of whom were clearly Asian. Eventually we trudged back to the RV.

"It is so pity—no moose," Angela told me. "But the world is so small. I meet three groups of Chinese, come from Texas and Taiwan and Hong Kong, but born in Shanghai so they can speak with me."

On we drove, with Angela's attempts to use the park map hindered by Lady's insistence on watching for wildlife from her lap.

Once we found our campsite, I planned the evening activities: an early supper, then check out likely moose habitat and attend the evening campfire talk in our campground. We actually got a glimpse of a female moose, browsing in Willow Flats near Jackson Lake Lodge, through a ranger's scope.

"The most important thing and the most exciting thing for us is to see the moose in the almost late afternoon," Angela said later. "Very short, and after we see that the moose is disappearing, so most visitors they don't get a chance to see the moose. So we are so lucky, so thank You, Lord, thank You to give us a chance to see the moose so quickly!"

Our campground ranger had a blaze going in the fire pit when we got to the amphitheater. A couple of families were equipped with sharp sticks and the makings of s'mores.

"Marsh mean wet ground, and mellow mean calm and quiet. Why they call it that?"

And, later, "Why they burn the candy?"

We could easily have spent a week or more in the Tetons, but our goal was Yellowstone, so we were up and out early in the morning.

Cows and buffalo

Before we left, we walked Lady around the KOA, stopping to look at several herds of cattle in fields on the edge of the park. Lady got to sniff at a calf, and Angela heard the "cry" of the cows.

"Buffalo … cow … no difference to me," she said confidently.

One reason for staying at a KOA is that many tour drivers will pick you up at the campground. So we left the air conditioning on for the animals and climbed into our tour minibus at the campground office. Driving into the park, we saw many, many bison—on the side of the road, on the hillsides, in the fields, in the road itself. At one point we saw a family group, including a calf.

"Buffalo … cow … different!" Angela exclaimed.

Our guide told us one could drive all 300 miles of Yellowstone roads, seeing everything one can see from the road, and still have seen only 2% of the park.

"When I see this kind of beauties—the big waterfalls, cascades, and those different geysers—I have no words to say. I don't think any language can describe such kind of beauty," Angela exclaimed. "It's incredible. It's amazing. We are so blessed to enjoy every masterpiece God has made!"

Angela asked several times, "Who take care of animal? And tree? Who feed animal?"

The guide and I explained that this was a natural area. The rangers are there primarily to protect the animals and plants from the people.

"As a Chinese, I just really feel surprised when I see a national park and everything is keeping in the natural way," Angela elaborated. "And I can imagine it's very difficult. It's open to the public and the people, so not only ranger, but also the visitors, everyone needs to preserve, protect the natural."

Poop

I parked my RV at Old Faithful so we could see the geysers. Suddenly Angela stopped, in the middle of the parking lot.

"Oh," she said, "look! That where you go when you need comfort?"

"Um, no, it's a bathroom, actually. We do have funny names for bathrooms in English—comfort station, powder room, john, even bathroom isn't what it's really for."

Angela laughed. "In China we call it WC."

We arrived at West Thumb in time to join a ranger with a group of tourists. We saw elk and bison scat, and the ranger asked, "Does anyone know what scat is?"

Most people giggled, and the children called out, "Poop!"

"That's right," the ranger responded, and taught us a helpful rhyme:

It starts with S and ends with T.
It comes out of you, and it comes out of me.
Now wait, don't say it—it could be that,
But we'll be scientific, and we'll call it scat!

And the tour went on—leaving me to define *poop* for Angela.

Bears

We took another guided tour the next day, looping the top half of the park. This guide was an expert bear finder. He took us to what he called the "Bear-muda Triangle" where, in the course of the day, we sighted a total of twelve bears, including two sets of twin cubs.

"This is my first time to see bears, elks, deers, antelopes, coyotes, in an open space. I feel people stand by and just watch them and not bother them, so I highly appreciate Americans do that," Angela told me that evening. "Animals just live in the same natural, and it's fair we should be friendly to every animal because they are God's property, no matter they are predators or kind animals, no matter they look pretty and lovely, or they look ugly or unattractive."

On our way home, I asked Angela what she thought of America's first and best-known national park.

"I hope every visitor when they have vacation will come to the national park and not only just for fun or to relax," she said. "It's a real good chance for them to enjoy the nature and to get involved into the nature, to appreciate the nature which is all of God's property and belong to God."

Been there—done that—got the T-shirt? Now my eyes were opened to the true wonder of Yellowstone, because I was given the privilege of viewing it through eyes that showed me a different perspective. Try traveling with Angela if you doubt me.

Chapter 34: Your RV Toolbox
Fun and Games with the Kids

Chores and License Plates

A few suggestions for keeping the children happy on the road.

"Don't you need gas, Elsi? Or a bathroom stop?"

"No, I'm just fine. Why?"

"'Cause you said we got a present when you stop. And I know which one I want!"

My RV was new, and so was the concept of traveling with my friend and her children. Searching for ways to minimize the brother-sister squabbles often arising from boredom, I re-created a game my grandmother had made for me almost five decades earlier.

I bought dozens of small "trip gifts"—little dolls, coloring and sticker books, handheld games, books of facts or jokes, card games, simple puzzles, key chains, packages of car activities. The wrapping was color-coded: blue for teenage Ryan, pink for six-year-old Emily, and yellow for things they could share.

Then I generated a list: first gas stop, time zone change, an hour after lunch, when we had spotted 15 different state license plates, and so forth. I tagged a few packages: "save for campground" on pool toys; "for Elsi and Mom, too" on jokes and travel games.

Ryan and Emily seemed to enjoy being included in RV life. Of course, we paid for chores, which kept their interest up. We kept track of points earned and chores done by each child. The door of my RV fridge was a whiteboard, and I brought dry erase markers, so we had a visual reminder of how we were doing.

"Point for Ryan for letting Emily nap."

"Point for Emily for not whining."

Each point was worth a dime.

Chores included helping with meals, helping connect and disconnect in the campground, taking out the trash, and similar "housekeeping" activities. Each was worth a quarter.

This gave the kids spending money for gift shops as well as providing motivation for cooperation and helpfulness. In my rig, by the way, gift shops do not happen until *after* the activity connected with the shop has been completed. On the way out of the park, after touring the zoo, when we've seen the museum—then you can go to the gift shop.

In addition to regular car games and collecting state license plates, we played several alphabet games. I find those so much fun that I play them by myself when I'm out on my own. The simplest, of course, is spotting the letters in order on signs. But my favorite is Bible alphabet.

"A is for animal, because Noah took animals on the ark."

You can increase the challenge level by requiring a visual connection.

"I see bushes in that field. God talked to Moses in a burning bush."

"I see a car, like when God drove Adam and Eve out of Eden."

"Hey! That's cheating!"

"Yeah, but it's funny!"

Collections

I collect hatpins for my trip hat. Before I retired, I used those hats to teach geography and history to my elementary school students. I would toss the hats on children's desks when we were waiting for buses or lunch, the kids would look at the pins and ask questions, and I'd tell the stories behind the pins.

Ryan tried getting patches from each site, then pens. He wanted to start a knife collection, but you can't afford that at 25¢ a chore.

Emily collected rocks. Preferably the garish ones you buy by the bag in gift shops, but she also enjoyed interestingly colored ones on beaches. We strictly enforced the law prohibiting taking natural items in the national parks, of course.

As we left Petrified Forest National Park, a ranger asked, "Does anyone have any rocks?" Knowing what he meant, Diane and I said, "No."

But Emily's eyes got big, and she solemnly showed him her bags of purple and orange stones. He praised her honesty and said she could keep them.

"Look at this book about rocks," Diane said to Emily after a couple of years of this. "You could learn the names of your rocks."

"I know their names," Emily said certainly. Did we have a budding geologist on our hands?

"This one," she said, picking up a green stone with orange specks, "is Cassandra. And this one is … Ralph."

I chose campgrounds with activities for the kids: we swam every night, rented bikes, played miniature golf, and allowed Ryan to check game scores on the rec room TV.

When Ryan demanded equal time in the front seat, I insisted that the person in the navigator's seat had to follow the map and itinerary, as well as amuse me with conversation or games.

We could separate the children into different areas when necessary. Often one or the other would head for the bed to take a nap or read. Emily would play with her stuffed animals, and Ryan took to lying on the bed with my binoculars, watching traffic behind us, trying to spot different license plates.

Every night, when I was typing up the trip log on my laptop, I asked my passengers to share what they remembered about the day's activities. This interactive trip log made a great addition to my photographs.

Personal favorites

As Emily and Ryan have grown older, they have become less interested in toys along the way and more intrigued by special activities. Ryan wants to watch "the game" on TV in the campground game room. And Emily plans movie nights, with a choice of DVDs (we generally have to compromise) and a big bowl of popcorn (another of the cat's favorite toys).

Another way we've developed to keep the peace is to ensure that each person gets to choose one activity as a "personal favorite." On our Yellowstone trip, Ryan wanted to see bears, and I wished for a moose. Emily's heart was set on a horseback ride, and their mom requested "half an hour of peace by a river."

We took a breakfast trail ride near Yellowstone, and I saw a moose in the Tetons. We detoured into Idaho for Ryan's bears, stopping at Yellowstone Bear World.

On our way home, we camped by a fast-flowing stream. After supper, Diane sat on the bank, toes in the cool water.

"Come on, Mommy! I want to swim!" Emily begged.

"Ryan, will you swim with her?" Diane asked.

"Aw, Mom!" Ryan protested.

"But I want *you!*" Emily complained.

"Wait a minute," I said. "Em, we all had a great time riding the horses yesterday. And it was so much fun this morning, tossing apples to the wolves and bears! I even got to see a moose! All Mom wanted was a quiet time by a stream."

"Oh."

"Okay."

And the three of us had a pleasant evening at the pool. When Diane joined us, her face was relaxed, and she was humming.

We each managed something special, and it felt good to all of us.

Tools for Keeping the Kids Happy

- Bring treats and games
- Suggest the children start a collection
- Do "junior ranger" activities in parks
- Enlist the children's suggestions for activities and stops
- Give grace; be patient—you too were young once

Travel Is Pretty Simple
<u>Six TIPS for Car Games (no supplies needed, one or more players)</u>

1. Spot the letters of the alphabet on billboards. This game can be played as a contest (one side of the road against the other, for example) or as a group activity (how fast can the whole group working together complete the alphabet), or by an individual playing alone.

    Two sources—
    1.   on billboards and vehicle signs
    2.   on license plates

2. Topical alphabet

    Name/explain things in alphabetical order and on a chosen topic:
    1.   Songs (first line or title): "Amazing Grace"; "Bingo Was His Name-O"
    2.   Things you see along the way: ads, billboards, cat on porch
    3.   Things from the Bible: Adam, Babylon, cross
    4.   Animal names or traits: ants, birds, cawing crows
    5.   Things you're glad for: answered questions, babies, chewing gum
    6.   Whatever you can think of

3. Other alphabet games

    1.   I packed my grandmother's trunk, and in it I put an aardvark; I packed my grandmother's trunk, and in it I put an aardvark and a balloon; …
    2.   My name is Adele; I come from Africa; I like appetizing apples. My name is Bob; I come from Burbank; I like brilliant borders.…

4. Singing games

    1.   Songs on a topic: animals, places, sounds, water, …
    2.   Songs including a certain word: big, car, …
    3.   Songs about things you see out the windows

5. Rhyming games

    1.   Spot something, name it, and give a rhyme: tree:see
    2.   Spot something and make a rhyming couplet: That is a tree. I wish I could ski.
    3.   Match lines: first player gives a first line; next player makes a rhyming line; continue until someone misses. Then start a new one: That is a car. It came from far. Twinkle twinkle little star. Jelly is in a jar. I fell down and hurt myself and it left a scar.

6. Geography

First player says a word that would be on a map, for example, Mississippi.

Next player must give a map word that starts with the last letter of the previous word: Illinois.

Singapore. Europe. East. Timbuktu. Uganda....

Words may not be repeated.

Caveat: A lot of words both begin and end with A (Australia, America ...)

Chapter 35: Your RV Toolbox
Educational Activities Along The Way

You're Trying to Teach Us Something!

Making the trip count, for students and other learners

"No, I won't give you real dollars for this money. But you can shop each Friday in the room for real stuff."

My group of learning-disabled fifth and sixth graders still used their fingers to add or subtract, had no idea why anyone would ever want to do math, and thought they were total failures at it. So, why should they bother trying?

I put together a checkbook behavioral program. I made positive and negative tally marks on a card for each child, and those translated into "dollars" for their class bank account. Each Friday, they could write checks to "buy" toys and candy with the "money" they had earned by good behaviors. It was an enormous amount of work on my part, but it paid off in better class attitude and actions. And, I hoped, it taught them about checking accounts and budgeting.

One day I was moving around the table, making tally marks and saying such things as, "Nice job, Bill!"

"Good work, Troy!"

"I like the way you're thinking, Jenny!"

"Boy, you're sure working hard, Carl!"

Jessica stopped in the middle of her problem and watched me. Then, in a tone of disgust, she stated, "*I* know what *you're* doing! You're trying to *teach* us something!"

Are you hoping to teach your children something as you travel? Maybe you are homeschooling, or perhaps you just want vacations to be useful as well as fun. There are two basic ways to make this work: pick a theme and travel it, or plan a trip and find educational connections.

Themes and connections

You can pick a topic from your child's curriculum for the next year, or choose a passion area. Then plan your trip around that theme.

You can follow the Lewis and Clark trail, track Sacagawea across the Northwest, or visit Civil War sites. You can learn about government by visiting state and national capitols and courthouses.

Homeschooling friends of mine researched dolphins (their daughter's passion), then visited Discovery Cove in Orlando, Florida, where the whole family swam with the dolphins.

You can track an author's life and books. Gene Stratton-Porter (*Freckles* and *Girl of the Limberlost*) lived in California as well as Indiana; Ralph Moody (*Little Britches*) wrote about both Massachusetts and Colorado. The family of Laura Ingalls Wilder (*Little House*) traveled around the country before she and her husband settled in southwest Missouri.

Study dinosaurs on Canada's dinosaur trail and Utah's Dinosaur National Park. Research native and ethnic instruments through Appalachia and the West. Pick an art or a craft and see what's being done with it in each area you visit.

Visit Paul Bunyan sites in Minnesota, and read tall tales. Examine the history of a cultural group, a church, or an area. Compare mountain ranges; investigate how rivers change; follow our nation's explorations in space; learn about captive breeding of endangered species.

Heading for California? Study the gold rush, or fruit. Connecticut? How about whales, or sailing ships? Missouri has Mark Twain and Eugene Field, as well as the Dred Scott slavery case (did you know Dred Scott's lawyer was Eugene Field's father?).

My search for autumn color in the Midwest includes several authors: Laura Ingalls Wilder, Jan Karon, Bess Streeter Aldrich, and Gene Stratton Porter. My visit to Maine will include many authors along the way, as well as the Johnstown Flood Museum and quite a few tourist trains.

Include your student

Your children can help plan the trip by reading tour guides and highlighting places they are interested in. Older students can get information from the Web, write or phone for further information, mark maps, and figure out a general plan for each day.

When I did a Midwest trip with friends, one of the girls, eleven, had never read the *Little House* books. I provided *Little House on the Prairie* on tape so she would understand what we were doing.

During the trip, children can journal or take notes for family journaling, take pictures and keep a photo log, or draw pictures of what you're seeing. They can help keep track of the budget, navigate, take notes for reports to be done later in the school year, or help monitor the exchange rate between Canada and the United States.

They can follow your route on maps with a highlighter, note elevation and weather changes, observe environment and animals, and follow the Continental Divide. It's just a few years ago that I discovered that Canada and Alaska have *triple* continental divides, where water flows to the Pacific, Atlantic, and Arctic oceans.

Each person can choose or create a persona to travel with. On my Utah trip with friends, I became "Pa" (don't ask), while my friend's teenage son was "Young'un." We were in a covered wagon and had to take care of the animals and "wimmin folk."

Some children might want to look at your journey from the point of view of a hobbit or someone from Star Wars. Jan Karon wrote a book about a traveling stuffed bunny (*Jeremy: Tales of an Honest Bunny*), which might inspire younger children.

You can find songs or stories from each area by contacting local libraries or checking for songbooks in Visitor Centers. Choose an animal to follow across the country. Collect legends from different regions. Take notes on plants, birds, and food, and how those vary as you move across the country. Even a very young Emily understood that everything we did needed to be about the trip; she bought a toy dog and named it Penny, "because we're in D.C. and Lincoln's statue is here too and Lincoln's picture is on the penny!"

In the fine arts, you can take pictures, draw or paint, find area coloring books, collect postcards, read stories and poems and songs.

There's almost no end to educational opportunities while you're having fun on the road.

Tools for Educational Opportunities

- Pick a theme
- Find connections
- Include your student
- You can learn, too

Chapter 36: Trip Commentary
My Midwest Author Loop

Traveling and Reading

Author tours aren't only for kids.

By fourth grade I had read all of Laura Ingalls Wilder's *Little House* books. I ignored the history and geography and missed the autobiography, but eagerly absorbed the happy family united against the perils of the frontier.

In addition to her *Little House* books, there are collections of her essays and articles from local newspapers, books by her daughter, Rose Wilder Lane, and *Farmer Boy*, about her husband's childhood. Written in the early 1900s, the books are set primarily in the middle to late 1800s. They tell about a pioneer family's travels and follow Laura from toddler to wife and mother.

About sixth grade, burrowing in the attic, I discovered a box of my mother's childhood books. Here were her copies of the *Pooh* books … *Treasure Island* … *Elsie Dinsmore* (which I liked primarily because I shared the heroine's first name) … a horrible little story about the importance of dental hygiene called, I believe, *Just 10 More Minutes*. And, best of all, battered editions of *Freckles*, *Girl of the Limberlost*, and *Laddie*, all by Gene Stratton Porter. With or without families, the young people in Porter's books stood firm against evil and thoughtlessness, joining with the forces of nature to grow up strong and happy.

Written and set in the early 1900s, the books weave the story into a natural setting, presenting animals, plants, and birds as a strong force in people's lives. *Freckles* and *Girl of the Limberlost* are a set; the others stand alone. Most take place in the swamplands of northern Indiana, though two (*Her Father's Daughter* and *Keeper of the Bees*) occur in California and *Michael O'Halloran* is based in and around Chicago. Porter was a nature photographer and published many books of natural science.

Reading a tour guide as part of my vacation planning as an adult, I found to my surprise and delight that the Limberlost was a real place in Indiana. Through the years I had found a few other titles by Gene Stratton Porter but knew nothing about her as a person or author.

I was astounded when I arrived at the "Cabin in Wildflower Woods" near Rome City, Indiana. It was the Bird Woman's house, and Gene herself, I soon discovered, was the real Bird Woman. On a chair was Little Sister's doll, and

Elnora's violin was on a shelf. I could not have been more startled and thrilled had I stepped into a wardrobe, parted the coats, and found myself in Narnia.

I walked the woods, discovering the copy of Little Sister's playhouse where Laddie wooed the Princess, and the very spot from which the Harvester saw his love walking on the moonlight across the lake. In my nearby campground I lifted the cover of the power box to plug in my RV and saw an enormous moth, just like the ones Elnora collected to pay her school expenses.

Another author whose home I enjoy visiting is Bess Streeter Aldrich. I must have been in junior high when I first read her book *Lantern in Her Hand*. Similar to the *Little House* books in that the family was establishing a home in the frontier wilderness, *Lantern* was written from the point of view of an adult instead of a child, but I enjoyed it anyway.

Bess Streeter Aldrich is also known for *Miss Bishop*; a movie was made from that story. Her books, written in the mid-1900s, present a picture of pioneer Nebraska. Several of the books are collections of stories.

Living and writing within a hundred years of one another, Aldrich, Wilder, and Porter have notable similarities. The most obvious is their double names. Not the playful, cultural double names of Lucy Maude Montgomery, author of the *Anne of Green Gables* series—my mother was Molly Jean all her life, although I was Elsi Jean only when I was naughty. Each of these women kept her maiden name as a middle name, showing a sense of family so strong they could not deny their family of origin. This connection with family is strongly emphasized in their stories and books.

A desire to explain their own families, plus the need to teach others, shows throughout the books, also. Wilder is, of course, the Laura of the stories. She fictionalized her life only slightly, omitting and combining incidents for improved story-telling. Aldrich was not herself a pioneer in the westward movement, but her ancestors were, and she tells their story. Porter is the Bird Woman of *Freckles* and *Girl of the Limberlost*. Wilder and Aldrich specifically wanted younger generations to know the history of their area; Porter hoped people would read her stories and learn about nature.

Later I added the real Limberlost cabin in Geneva, Indiana, just south of Rome City, to my itinerary. On that trip, looking for a different route to Indiana from Colorado, I also drove through southern Missouri and stopped at Laura Ingalls Wilder's adult home in Mansfield.

It is 650 miles from the Aldrich home in Elmwood, Nebraska, to Porter's homes in western Indiana. To Wilder's adult home in Mansfield, Missouri is another 650 miles. A shorter distance, 350 miles, takes you from southwest Missouri to southeast Nebraska, back to Aldrich's home. In a loop of only about 1,600 miles you can cover all three authors, with the possibility of adding Willa Cather, Eugene Field, Mark Twain, extra Wilder and Porter homes, and several delightful zoos.

Of course, you can choose any subject and read about it. You can choose a topic or era and travel to places important to it. You can visit the Mississippi River while reading *Tom Sawyer*, Atlanta while studying and reading about the Civil War, and numerous Lewis and Clark sites. But touring author sites is special, somehow.

There's something about being able to say, "I saw Pa's violin."

Or "And there was Little Sister's doll."

"I've been in Injun Joe's cave."

"You can see from these pictures why Anne loved the open spaces."

"No wonder Jesse Stuart wanted to help the poor people of these mountains!"

"Field's house seems designed for a child to play in."

"It sounds easy, but look at how long the bridge actually is!"

"The people are still so poor; it's easy to see why they needed a shepherd, a friend."

Can you match the comments above to their books and areas?

The violin, from Wilder's *Little House* books, is in her home in Mansfield, Missouri. Little Sister's doll is from Porter's *Laddie* and can be found in her home in Rome City, Indiana. Tom Sawyer and Becky Thatcher were lost in Injun Joe's cave in Hannibal, Missouri, home of Mark Twain. Anne's Green Gables are on Prince Edward Island, where Lucy Maude Montgomery wrote the *Anne of Green Gables* series. Jesse Stuart worked his way through school to become a teacher in Appalachian Kentucky. Eugene Field wrote "Wynken, Blinken, and Nod" and other poems; his childhood home is now a toy museum in St. Louis. The railroad bridge Kate Shelley crossed to save a train in a storm is near Boone, Iowa. John Fox's *Little Shepherd of Kingdom Come* and Harold Bell Wright's *Shepherd of the Hills* feature poverty-stricken mountain people, in Kentucky and Missouri respectively.

By visiting an author's home with your family or students, you provide that hands-on connection with a book or series that produces dedicated readers. And for yourself? An intimate connection with an author and his or her books. It can't be beat!

Chapter 37: Your RV Toolbox
Traveling with a Dog and a Cat

The Magic RV

Some simple preparations and precautions will let you include your furry friends in your vacation.

My gray tabby, Dolphin, leaps to the dashboard as I switch on the windshield wipers. Eyes and ears move with the wiper blades. When he knows the pattern, his tail tip starts to twitch slowly. Then he pounces, swiping wildly with his paws. Of course, he is on the other side of the glass from the blades, but that doesn't bother him. He is sure they are the wings of magic birds and if he catches one, he just might get a wish.

When the rain stops, he sits a moment longer, watching the windshield. Then he hops to the floor and strides off. The birds have stopped flapping their wings, and he is a conqueror.

Dolphin has been traveling in the RV since he was a kitten, so he feels it is his home. My previous cat, who went wild in a moving car, seemed unaware that my rig moved. I think she thought I had two houses, a big one and a small one.

There's a popular series of children's books (by Mary Pope Osborne) about a magic tree house that travels in time and space. Lady, my beagle, thinks we have a magic RV. She leaps into our little house and naps on the sofa. When the door opens, she is in a new place, with fresh smells and new people to pat her.

I am out for weeks, sometimes months at a time. I don't travel with tour groups or caravans, and I would be lonely without Lady and Dolphin to keep me company, help me check out parks and campgrounds, and provide opportunities for pictures and conversation along the way.

Food and comfort

Traveling with my animals is safer and more comfortable for them than if they were in a kennel. They not only provide company for me, they give me a measure of security, also. Walking Lady is a safe way to met strangers, and no one would know her wild barking at the door is Lady's way of saying, "Hello, you adorable serial murderer—pat me!"

Since the world revolves around Lady (just ask her), she is not surprised to find that people drive from all over the United States for the privilege of patting her.

Some of them come to gas stations; others, to campgrounds or tourist attractions; quite a few show up at highway rest stops. Workers at tollbooths, service station attendants, picnickers … Lady knows the only reason they are there is so they can pat her. I stopped for a picture of the welcome sign at the Alaska state line, a tour bus behind me. Lady placed herself at the foot of the bus steps, eagerly greeting each of the 40 people on the bus.

It isn't hard to provide the amenities my animals need in our RV. I keep an old towel by the door for muddy paws after walks, along with Lady's leash and bags and Dolphin's harness and leash. Dolphin's litter box is in the shower stall on a rug, with a baby gate across the doorway. His food dish is on a skid-proof mat on the counter, along with his water dish, an unspillable one from an RV store.

We have developed a few rules for happy traveling: You may not sit on my lap when I'm driving. Do not walk under my accelerator foot. Please don't jump on my head. Rules are not always enough, especially for a cat. Dolphin enjoys opening the cab windows by walking on the switches, so I put duct tape over them. And I had to replace the kitchen faucet handle, which pushed up; Dolphin kept walking under the old one and turning on the water.

As long as she has supper on time and new patters available, Lady is happy. (Of course, she does prefer that I not touch the brakes unless I'm stopping, as it interrupts her sleep.) And she seldom objects to having her leash tied to a post so I can get a picture with some "human" interest.

IDs

Neither Dolphin nor Lady would ever leave me on purpose. However, once they spot or smell something interesting, they forget that I can't run at their speed. Therefore, each of them has an ID chip inserted by my vet. Any vet or shelter that finds them will scan for the chip. My service then calls both my vet and me. Before I leave, I make sure my vet knows how to get in touch with me when I'm gone.

Many pet stores sell inexpensive ID tags, and for longer trips I make one with a friend's phone number on it. I have also found temporary, barrel-shaped tags, with a slip of paper for traveling information inside. I use these options just in case the finder doesn't take my animal to a vet.

My vet's name and phone number are on my emergency contact card in my wallet and glove compartment. And, since most campgrounds now have accessible modem connections, I can be reached by e-mail in an emergency.

Health and safety

The animals are perfectly happy in the RV when I'm out being a tourist. With the windows open, the RV is comfortable, even in the sun in the Midwest, though I try to park in shade, of course. I use the air conditioner when I'm in a campground; in a parking lot, it's not a good option. When I'm on an all-day tour, there is always someone at the RV park or tourist attraction desk who will be delighted to walk the dog at lunchtime for a tip. At Denali National Park in Alaska, Lady got hourly walks all day. Parked in a boat cruise lot, I asked a girl in a nearby ice cream shop to check on Lady for me. She was glad to earn extra money by taking Lady out and giving her some attention.

Heartworm medication is crucial for traveling into mosquito territory (almost all the United States, nowadays), and I add flea/tick repellent when we go south or east. The cat gets that, too, much against his better judgment. I keep the animals' shots up-to-date anyway, but I make sure to have a health certificate with me when I'm on the road.

On my Alaska trip I crossed international borders several times. At each crossing I opened my window to hand the customs official my driver's license and passport, health certificates for both animals, and my RV registration and insurance papers. Each time Lady leapt into my lap and requested petting from the officer.

At one border, the officer was rubbing Lady's ears while he asked a string of questions, "Do you have any firearms in your RV?"

"No, sir."

"Illegal drugs?"

"No."

"Any plants?"

"No."

"Anything with fur?"

"Sir, you are petting the only fur-bearing item in my rig."

Dolphin meowed a protest as the official laughed. And I drove my magic RV across the border, knowing that Dolphin would enjoy stalking Canadian dinosaurs and Lady would find lots of new beagle-patters, eh?

Tools for Keeping Happy Four-Footed Friends

- Have enough pet food for the trip (and buy it ahead of time, at home).
- Remember treats and chews.
- Check that the water dish is full, secure, and not going to splash.
- Bring toys, if your pet needs them.
- Carry any medication animals might need, and copies of prescriptions.
- Ask your vet about an ID chip, heartworm prevention, and flea/tick prevention.
- Bring a health certificate if you're leaving the country.
- Have a way for your vet to reach you in an emergency.

Travel Is Pretty Simple
Four TIPS on the Advantages of Traveling with Your Pet

1. You're not paying for a kennel.
2. They're good company (most of the time).
3. Walking a dog (or cat!) is a great way to start a conversation.
4. They're warm in bed.

Chapter 38: Side Trip to Mitchell, South Dakota
June 2006

Love across the Picnic Table

My cat fell in love with a kitty in a neighboring camper.

Do you remember those brief, intense summer romances? You saw a cute boy at the lake … an adorable girl showed up at the pool … it was love at first sight. You two were meant for each other, parting reluctantly and with tearful vows of eternal fidelity as your cruel families drove in opposite directions at the end of the week.

Well, Dolphin fell in love at the KOA in Mitchell, South Dakota. I was up about 2 AM and noticed him on the back of the chair, nose to the screen, talking. It wasn't his "bird" noise, nor a warning of incoming dinosaurs. He was meowing in a conversational tone.

I looked out the window and discovered a Class C rig had pulled in after I'd gone to bed. On the dashboard was a petite, orange-and-cream-striped cat. Her nose was pressed against the driver's window, and I could see her mouth moving. When I got up for breakfast, Dolphin was still at his post, meowing sweet nothings to her through the window.

Later I met the kitty's papa and arranged to come a-visiting. He had noticed Dolphin, paw on the screen, communing with Sunny-Cat, *aka* Sunshine. Sunny and her family were affiliated with the military and had been transferred to Wisconsin from Washington. We chatted and I patted Sunny; then they came over to my RV and we talked while they patted Lady and attempted to stroke Dolphin.

"She can't," the man told me, "but wouldn't they have adorable kittens?"

I agreed. Dolphin hasn't met another cat since he was a baby in the pet store, and I didn't dare trust his self-restraint enough to risk letting the two meet.

As Sunny's rig pulled out of the campground, he stayed on his chair, promising to e-mail Sunny when they were apart.

Chapter 39: Your RV Toolbox
Getting along with the Neighbors

… As Thyself …

Be patient. Be patient. But not too patient.

Neighbors are neighbors. Some are friendly, and some ignore you. Some have children who run through your yard scattering toys and litter; others' kids carefully put their candy wrappers in the trash. Some are noisy; others, quiet. It's just part of having neighbors, at home or in a campground. Of course, it's easier to be patient when you'll only have to cope with problems for one night. Nonetheless, as we tell parents, choose your battles—is this problem bad enough to justify making people angry?

Since bad experiences tend to be memorable, I can easily list a few bad neighbors I've had. My worst experience was probably July 4, 1999, in Michigan. It's far from typical, I'm sure, but I continued to admire their chutzpah even as I fumed at their rudeness.

I must admit, they were well organized. Sitting in my RV at the entrance to the campsite, I saw a playpen, two tethered puppies, a blanket covered with dolls and toy dishes, an enormous campfire laid in the fire pit, and a child riding a Big Wheel. The opening to the site was blocked by two parked cars.

I checked my map—I was definitely in the right place. I got out and knocked on RV doors and called, "Hello!" Surely someone was supervising that child and the dogs?

Eventually a man came from the beach across the road. "You need something?" he asked politely.

"Well, um, I've been assigned this campsite, and it seems to be occupied."

"Yeah, Bill and his family left this morning. But we just kept using it, since we're parked all around it. He told us we should."

I waited for him to offer to move the cars and let me in. When this didn't happen, I said, "The manager said this is my site, and there isn't another one I can switch to. Could you guys let me in, please?"

He stared at me in disbelief. Couldn't I see that they were putting the space to good use? I smiled and tried to look non-threatening. Finally he got the cars moved and corralled the child.

Uneasily, I backed into the portion of the campsite he had cleared. I plugged the RV in and walked Lady, noticing unfriendly stares from my neighbors. *Hey, it's not my fault.*

Through my windows I could see them gathering for supper. There were four family groups, with what must have been at least ten children and a couple more dogs. I had just started my own meal when Lady started baying in response to a knock on the door. It was my "friend" from next door.

"Thought you'd want to know," he said. "We're planning a big campfire this evening, right on your front bumper."

I expected him to invite me to attend—silly me. I waited. He waited.

"You know," I offered tentatively, "if you'd move the toys and stuff from behind my rig and help guide me under the trees, I could get farther away from your campfire."

He did this, and I backed away from the fire circle. As night fell and the group settled around their roaring fire, I closed my shades and turned the air conditioner fan to high.

It was a large fire, and they had to almost shout across it to their friends. They had plenty of beer and a swarm of happy children. Finally, in desperation, I put on a CD of "fireworks for symphonies." With the volume fairly high, I could block out enough of the noise so I could go to sleep, singing along with the choir.

In retrospect, I suppose I could have gone to the manager. But even though they were noisy well after quiet time, it was the Fourth of July, after all. I was able to get to sleep, and they were having so much fun!

To my amusement and further frustration, I had as much trouble leaving as I'd had getting into the site. I had to find adults to move the trucks they had blocked my exit with and ask their help in spotting my corners as I wended my way around their toys and piles of wood. I'm sure they were as relieved as I was when the campground was in my rearview mirror.

This time I went to the manager

Then there was a night in a Wyoming KOA, when the neighbor's dog barked non-stop from about 8:15 to almost 11 at night. Remembering my Fourth of July experience, I tried a CD and the fan. The dog kept barking. I could have turned the volume up more, but I was worrying about the dog. It had been alone in the rig for hours and was clearly unhappy.

So eventually I went to the manager to report the situation. I do want to be the kind of neighbor I try to have. And I'd rather people gave me some grace, or talked to me in person, than report me to the authorities. In this case, though, the people weren't home, and I would want someone to rescue my pets if I left them alone too long (if I were in an accident, for example).

The manager thanked me and asked me to put my complaint in writing, handing me pencil and paper on the spot. He explained that they had been getting complaints about that trailer for several days, but no one would give details or sign anything.

By the way, the couple in the trailer came home about 2 AM and put their dog in a portable kennel outside the trailer. I noticed them driving to the shower (about 30 steps from where we were parked) in the morning. They hadn't walked their animal when I left about 7:30 AM.

Other bad neighbors?

Not many, really. Crying babies. Noisy engines. RVs with a back-up beeper, such as I met on the way to Alaska. Noisy parties. Nothing major. Nothing I couldn't ignore, offer grace, and continue to enjoy my trip.

Campers are good people

Old sailing ships had figureheads—elaborately carved creatures, often women, on the very front of the ship. Dolphin often serves as my figurehead, sitting on the dashboard of my RV and watching the world go by. He's looking for predators, no doubt.

I often hear people laughing or commenting as they walk through the campground or parking lot. Occasionally a parent will lift a little person high, and Dolphin will play patty-cake for a few seconds.

In the Mount Shasta KOA in Washington, Dolphin was happily chasing a bug on the dashboard when a German girl spotted him. I heard her calling to her parents, apparently telling them about the *lustige kleine Katze* (funny little cat). Soon she had her whole family out to watch his antics. They stood by their rig, smaller children on the picnic table, laughing and talking. Dolphin ignored them.

I've really had lots of good neighbors—it's just that most of them don't make for interesting stories. However, my first season out, a man came shouting after me when I forgot to unplug my power cord before pulling out. I was grateful!

I never have a problem finding neighbors to spot me as I back into a campsite.

A kind man in the adjoining campsite held Lady's leash while I dealt with a stubborn faucet connection.

And two different sets of people, in two different campgrounds, recommended Cypress Hills Inter-Provincial Park in Alberta and Manitoba—a delightful place to camp.

I try to be the kind of neighbor I want to have. I try to be patient when my neighbors' style clashes with mine.

My experience has generally been, as Mother often said, that campers are good people. It's a good group to be part of.

Tools for Good Neighbor Relations

- If you have bad neighbors, try to deal with it—unless it's a matter of health and safety
- Be a good neighbor:
    - o Keep kids and pets under control.
    - o Observe posted quiet hours.
    - o Be careful about loud music and shouted conversations at any hour.
    - o Clean up any spills, and use a collar to keep sewer smells down.
    - o Throw all trash away as directed.
    - o Supervise your fire, and be sure to completely extinguish it before leaving.
    - o Do unto others as you would have them do unto you.

Chapter 40: Side Trip to Mitchell, South Dakota
June 2005

Songs around the Campfire

Most neighbors really are friendly.

On our evening walk, Lady and I dropped by the campsite next door to greet our neighbors. Two couples and a young teen, they were attempting to start a campfire. I watched in amazement as one of the men touched the flame of his lighter to the side of a two-foot chunk of two-by-four in the fire pit.

Everyone waited. The edge of the board blackened. He shifted his grip. The black spot got larger. Lady introduced herself around the circle.

"Come on!" complained the teen. "Let's get going!"

"Um, could I make a suggestion?" I asked tentatively.

"Please do!" one of the women answered.

"You might want to start with tinder and kindling," I said.

Then, in response to their blank stares, I added, "You know, smaller pieces of wood."

The boy and one of the women got up and started collecting sticks and pine needles. The fire builder removed his board for them to dump the results into the circle. Then he dropped the board on top of the pile and bent down to try again.

"Would you let an old Girl Scout show you a trick?" I asked.

"Sure!" the man said.

I handed Lady's leash to the nearest person and demonstrated how to prop the sticks against the board, forming a tiny lean-to. We shoved pine needles into the opening.

"Now, light the needles."

You'd think I'd performed a magic trick. The flaming needles ignited the kindling, and I added a couple of boards, accompanied by appreciative comments: "Wow! "That's great!" "Hey, cool!"

Passing by at the end of Lady's and my walk, I was pleased to see smiling people drinking coffee and roasting marshmallows, and one of the women busily distributing crackers and squares of chocolate.

"You're welcome to join us!" she offered.

"No, but thanks!"

Back in the rig I fixed our bedtime snacks, filling Dolphin's dish and hiding Lady's pills in treats before settling down with my book and a dish of sugar-free ice cream.

Tendrils of wood smoke drifted through the screens, bringing dreams of Scout canoe trips and songs around the campfire. It was a good evening.

I tell people traveling in my rig, "Don't leave any cabinets open, unless you want Dolphin nesting in your stuff."

Dolphin loved prowling through the bushes at Cypress Hills Inter-Provincial Park in Saskatchewan.

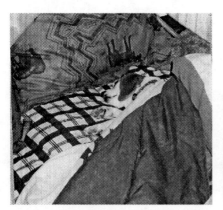

Lady is always happy to share space with visitors.

I visited the actual site of *Little House on the Prairie* with friends. Brittany and Chelsea enjoyed seeing the way pioneers lived.

→ *PART 5: THAT WAS FUN! NOW WHAT?*

Chapter 41: Your RV Toolbox
No Goldfish Moments

What Should I Do with All These Pictures and Fliers?

Some tips for easy ways to create a trip scrapbook

"Wow! There's a castle!" At the 2004 Oregon Christian Writer's Conference, one of the speakers, Karen Ball, told us that in their family it's not "a senior moment" but a "goldfish moment." Goldfish, she explained, have a 5-second memory loop, which is why "they can swim around that little bowl and say, 'Oh, look! It's a castle!' Another circuit, 'Hey! I've got a castle!'"

Goldfish moments—it sounds funny, and the story evokes laughter. However, by the time my grandmother was in her 90s, her memory was about gone, and there was nothing funny about it. Granny was the best grandmother a little girl could wish for. She loved me, and I missed her sharp sense of humor and mourned the loss of our relationship.

When we had moved her to a nursing home in her late 80s, I helped close up her house. Squirreled away in drawers and closets were all sorts of odd treasures: containers of prescription medication, unopened packages of underwear, a loaded pistol, and boxes of slides from her trip to Africa twenty years before.

In the box with her Africa pictures was the text of a talk she had given to women's groups and her high school students when she returned. I typed this up, integrating the pictures, as a Christmas present. I read her own words to her while she looked at the pictures—and she remembered!

My parents and I traveled extensively with a small trailer when I was a child. Each evening we wrote about the day in our trip log (these days, this would be called journaling). After my parents died, I found the stack of trip logs in a cabinet. Reading them brought back faded memories of the fun we shared.

When I travel, I consciously try to build future memories. I don't attempt fancy scrapbooks, but I make sure I have both words and pictures to describe my trips. *Some day*, I tell myself, *when I'm 96 and alone, the nurse will read to me from my albums, and I'll remember.*

Words and pictures

To that end, I journal daily while I'm on the road—under a tree while the animals play in the grass, at the dinette table, or curled comfortably on the sofa. I use my laptop to document activities, record comments or newly learned facts, and chat with the Lord about what happened.

I also carry a small notebook in my beltbag purse, so I can easily jot down information I don't want to lose. This is especially helpful for tours and day cruises. In Yellowstone, I kept a record of the bears we spotted (a full dozen, including two sets of twin cubs), along with an explanation of" nurse stumps" (new trees growing from the stumps of old ones), young trees growing best in the shade of a rock, and park history. If I'm carrying a second camera (a disposable for panorama shots, for example), I document my use of it. I learned that lesson when I got home from six weeks in and around Alaska, had my film developed, and realized I had twenty-four gorgeous, panoramic pictures of unidentified mountains. When I journal, I transfer my notebook thoughts to the computer.

"Would you take my picture?"

People are generally glad to help out, though I do have to explain to the younger ones, "You have to look through the little hole; there's no display or view screen."

Lady, my beagle, and I walked through the drizzle to the end of a "handicap accessible" trail (I wouldn't want to push a wheelchair up that incline). I stopped at the overlook to admire the rapids and rocks, with treed mountains behind them. After a few minutes, another intrepid walker came along.

"Will you take my picture?" I asked eagerly.

I showed him how to use my camera ("look through that little hole and push this button"), picked Lady up, and smiled.

"Why don't you put the dog on the railing?" he suggested.

"No, thanks!" I held Lady a bit more tightly until I could set her safely down and retrieve my camera.

Hmph! The idea!

At Klootchy Creek, Oregon, a Lewis and Clark Trail site, I saw the world's largest Sitka spruce. I took a picture of the tree, but all you can see is that it fills the frame. Another is aimed straight up through the branches. But the most telling picture is of Lady and me by the trunk, which stretches far to each side. That gives perspective for the other shots.

I travel for a week every summer with a friend and her children. Diane and I have developed a couple of personal rules for taking pictures. Rule #1: No butt shots. Rule #2: No baby goats.

Perhaps I should explain about the baby goats. Our first year out, Diane's daughter was going into first grade. We visited Bryce Canyon National Park, and our campground had a goat-feeding area. You know the type—lots of pregnant goats and baby goats and little machines that give you a few kibbles of goat food when you put in your quarter. Emily was tiny, blonde, utterly adorable. Any baby animal is cute, and baby goats are especially endearing. Emily feeding baby goats—priceless!

Diane and I stood, side by side, each with our own camera, and took pictures. Pictures of Emily inserting her quarter in the machine. Pictures of goats flocking around her. Pictures of baby goats with their little hooves on her chest, reaching for food. Pictures of Emily kissing baby goats on their little noses. We all had a wonderful time.

When we returned home, Diane and I got twin prints of our film, so we could share with each other. This is how Diane and I each ended up with thirty-eight pictures of Emily and the baby goats.

It's also when I learned that it's okay to cut a photograph. We wanted pictures of small Emily and small goats; the barn and dust and feeding trough and fence weren't important.

"No baby goats," therefore, has a couple of meanings. The first is that we do not take identical pictures. Emily has tweaked this one so that, when we visited the Oregon Trail Ruts in Guernsey, Wyoming, we produced a trio of shots for my album: a picture I took of Diane, who was taking a picture of Emily, who was taking a picture of me.

We also use "baby goats" as a code for "you're taking too many pictures of this."

Photo albums

I have an "old lady's camera," with film in it, the kind a friend calls a "poke and shoot" camera. My digital is too slow for eagles flying overhead, views from the train window, or the flash of a whale's tail. I buy film in bulk at a discount warehouse; it is atrociously expensive at tourist sites. When I finish a roll, I put the used film in the plastic container the new roll came in. On the container I write, in fine-tip permanent marker, the date and last activity: "8/7 sunrise" or "7/3 train Rainier." I keep the completed rolls in a bag till the end of my trip, and I make sure my cat cannot get at the bag.

When I take all my film to be developed, I copy the information from the container onto the envelope. That way I can easily put my pictures in order when I get them back.

I read my trip log while looking through the pictures. If I have a photograph of something I didn't journal about, it's easy to add the incident. Then I insert page breaks, so there's room for the pictures, and print my trip log.

I'm not at all artistic, so my albums aren't fancy. I use scrapbook paper and stickers—I especially enjoy national park and state stickers and tags. I save memorabilia—ticket stubs, programs, fliers and other informational handouts, even postcards—to include in my photos and journaling.

I add comments in pen, too: "baby goats here"; "Lady says, let's keep moving!"; "can you find the mountain goat?"

Sometimes I'll type out a song or hymn I'm fond of and match pictures to the words. Since I spend a lot of time on the road either singing or listening to CDs, those add to the flow of my trip narrative.

All those things bring back memories of my last trip, my trips last year, my trips and activities through the past several years … no more goldfish moments for me!

Tools for Memory Makers

- Carry a variety of cameras:
  - regular camera
  - disposable backup
  - kids' disposable
  - panoramic
  - waterproof
- Pack extra film.
- Store a small pocket notebook and pen in your purse, pack, or whatever you carry.
- Have a plan to store fliers, tickets, etc.
- Use a laptop or journal to keep track of what you do each day.

Travel Is Pretty Simple
Eight TIPS for Simple and Useful Memory Books after the Trip

1. Take a framing or title shot: the outside of the building, the "welcome to XXX" sign, the entrance to the forest, …
2. Include people, pets, and yourself in pictures, for scale and interest.
3. Get some pictures of the entire family in special places; let the kids clown around.
4. Buy postcards for large scenery (mountains, ocean, Grand Canyon).
5. Include fliers, ads, tickets.
6. Journal daily, and add family comments about activities.
7. You can buy themed paper and stickers for the national parks, Disney Parks, and other popular attractions.
8. Create a theme for your trip: Fall Leaves, On the Beach, There and Back Again; buy paper and stickers that match your theme.

➜ RV Rules—
Ten TIPS and Tools

Number One: Have fun.

  That's why you're out there, right?

Number Two: Old and new.

  Feel free to return to places you enjoyed. Equally, feel free to visit new places.

Number Three: Lots to see.

  When you spot something interesting, stop and visit.

Number Four: Less is more.

  Don't rush to see everything available; relax!

Number Five: Stay alive.

  Follow all normal safety precautions, especially on the roads.

Number Six: Take pics.

  Lots and lots and lots of pictures! These are the basis for your memories.

Number Seven: Think of heaven.

  Look for beauty, goodness, and random acts of kindness.

Number Eight: Play it straight.

  Obey the laws. Follow the rules. Be a good neighbor.

Number Nine: Mine and thine.

  Everyone should be able to do something special during the trip.

Number Ten: Do it again.

  Don't spend money for just one weekend a season. You'll enjoy your rig more as it becomes more familiar. And, each time, remember Number One: *HAVE FUN!*

Emily was so cute! And the baby goats were adorable. Ryan enjoyed feeding them, too, and Diane and I took far too many pictures. "Baby goats" is now our code for, "You're taking too many pictures," as well as, "Don't stand next to me and take the same picture I'm taking, okay?"

I carry my laptop with me in the RV and journal daily. That way I can integrate my photos with my journal entries so I have a complete scrapbook. I also check e-mail when I'm on the road, which is what I'm doing here at one of the few "hot spots" at Canby Grove, at the Oregon Christian Writers Summer Conference.

Appendix A
Checklists, Tools, TIPS

Tools for Essential Identification
- Driver's license
- Vehicle registration and insurance
- Health insurance cards
- Passport if you're crossing a border (though it's a good ID under any circumstances)
- Pet health information
    - o Health certificate from your vet (required at the border)
    - o Prescriptions, medication
- Emergency contact card
- Medical information
    - o medication (prescriptions)
    - o medical insurance card, number
    - o allergies/sensitivities

Four Tips for Using This Book
1. You can start at the beginning and read straight through, enjoying the stories and learning as you go.
2. You can turn directly to the chapter(s) or section(s) that meet your need at the moment, reading the Toolbox and stories to find answers.
3. You can look in the index (page 197) for topics of interest.
4. However you approach the text, remember to use the appendices:
    a. Checklists, tools, and tips are collected in Appendix A (page 153) for easier reference
    b. Resources such as tour guidebooks and campground guides are listed in Appendix B (page 171)
    c. Contact information for tourist sites, clubs, authors, cities, and so forth are given alphabetically in Appendix C (page 173)
    d. A Glossary of terms used in the book is Appendix D (page 193). Be sure to use it when you wonder what in the world I'm talking about.

Tools for Choosing an RV
- Research styles of RVs.
    - http://changingears.com/rv-checklist-gettings-started.shtml
    - http://www.gorving.ca/rvtips.asp
    - http://www.rvlifemag.com/file313/choosingrv.html
    - http://www.rvknowhow.com/chooseright.html
- If you don't have experience, try some RV styles out by renting or borrowing.
- Talk to people who are using them (in campgrounds or on the sales lot).
- If you'll be pulling a trailer or 5th-wheel, make sure your tow vehicle is strong enough. Your vehicle manual will tell you how much weight you can pull; remember to factor in the weight of water, holding tanks, supplies, people, and so forth.
- Invest in emergency road service. Yeah, this belongs in the Safety section. But it's so important I can't leave it out here.

Five TIPS for Choosing Your RV
1. Comfort in bed is extremely important.
2. Privacy is necessary, for naps or changing clothes; do you need a door or curtain?
3. Make sure the beds will be big enough as your children grow up.
4. Be sure you can you manage the rig physically (hitching, towing, cranking up the roof).
5. Plan for whatever special needs you may have: an inverter, TV, carrying bikes, pet needs such as kitty litter, transporting pool toys, extra handrails.

Tools: Checklists for Outside and Inside Walk-Arounds
Checklist for the outside walk-around
_____ all hoses and cords stored safely
_____ awning put away
_____ all storage bays (the "basement") latched securely
_____ step put in (if it isn't automatic)
_____ slide-out in
_____ stove vent closed
_____ nothing on the picnic table
_____ nothing hanging from the trees
_____ nothing lying on the grass/cement/gravel/whatever
_____ one full circuit of the RV without seeing anything that needs to be taken care of

Checklist for the inside walk-around
_____ water tank levels checked—black, gray, and fresh
_____ enough propane
_____ enough gasoline
_____ slide-out in
_____ antenna down
_____ furnace or AC off
_____ water heater off
_____ water pump on
_____ fridge packed safely so things don't spill or break
_____ fridge set to automatic (or gas) so it will work when you disconnect
_____ all cabinet doors and drawers closed securely
_____ all surfaces free of things that will slide or roll
_____ laptop computer and printer in a safe place
_____ doors latched (open or closed) so they won't flap and slam
_____ vents closed
_____ beds and bedding put away
_____ trash taken out or stored away
_____ pet water dish secure and filled
_____ seatbelts fastened (for your passengers—and remember to fasten yours, too)
_____ door locked

Six TIPS for Dealing with Maintenance Emergencies
1. File notes from your walk-through at the time of purchase with your manuals.
2. Keep all those notes and manuals handy.
3. Ask questions when you're getting service: from the salesman, your service guys, tow truck drivers, other RVers.
4. Be prepared:
   a. Have flashlights in the RV.
   b. Use gloves and wear washable shoes when dumping holding tanks.
   c. Keep at least half a tank of gas at all times.
5. Have extra quilts for unexpectedly cold nights.
6. Have wet wipes available.

Nine TIPS for Using Your Mirrors

1. Set the driver's seat comfortably for the main driver first.
2. Don't try to adjust mirrors alone; have a helper outside the rig.
3. You should have two mirrors on each side: a regular, flat one; a curved, "spot" one.
4. Adjust each flat mirror
   a. So you can see just the edge of the side of the rig
   b. So you can see the lane next to you quite a way behind the rig
   c. So you can see the bottom back corner of the rig and the rear tire touching the road surface
   d. So you can see the lane marker stripe
5. Adjust each spot mirror
   a. So you can see just the edge of the side of the rig
   b. So you can see the lane next to you the length of the rig
   c. So you can see the bottom, back corner of the rig and the rear tire touching the road surface
   d. So you can see the lane marker stripe
6. Drive within the lane marker stripes; try to stay centered.
7. Don't change lanes if your spot mirror shows a vehicle.
8. Remember that your tail swings out when you turn.
   a. Watch your corners.
   b. Note where your rear tires are in relation to curbs and other hazards.
   c. Try to turn from an outside lane.
9. Many truckers will flash their lights when it's safe to pull in front of them when passing or changing lanes on the highway.
   a. If that's helpful to you, do it for other drivers, too.
   b. Blink your parking lights a couple of times to thank them.

Six TIPS for Converting to and from Metric

1. Use a conversion tool when you're planning: (http://www.psinvention. com/zoetic/convert.htm)
    a. There are other Web sites available, also.
    b. Visitor Centers near the border may have a conversion table for you.
2. Distance
    a. Indicate on your itinerary whether mileage is metric or American.
    b. Automobile speedometers are marked in both metric and American.
    c. Use your speedometer as a rough converter (since 50 mph=80 kph, then 50 miles is 80 km).
    d. For short distances, a meter and a yard are about equivalent
3. Money
    a. Ask at the border for the current exchange rate, which varies widely, even from day to day.
    b. Figure a simple and rough conversion so you can think about prices in stores ("about half" or "about one-and-a-half").
4. Gas
    a. Remember, English and metric gallons are not the same size.
    b. There are about 4 liters to an English gallon.
    c. I find it simplest not to try to convert liters/gallon to miles/gallon; there are too many variables.
5. Temperature
    a. The United States thinks in Fahrenheit (F). Canada thinks in Celsius (C).
    b. 5/9 (F-32)=C (subtract 32 from the Fahrenheit temperature; multiply the answer by 5/9). For a VERY ROUGH equivalent: F-30, take half of it (subtract 30 from the F temperature, then take half of that).
    c. (9/5 C) + 32 = F (multiply the Celsius temperature by 9/5, then add 32). For a VERY ROUGH equivalent: Twice C and add 30.
6. Your RV
    a. You may need to know your vehicle's height, width, and weight in metric.
    b. Your vehicle's data sticker will have the data listed both ways.
    c. Know your height and width without having to check when you come upon narrow lanes, overpasses, and so forth.

Tool: Sample Packing List

Clothes

slacks (2)	long-sleeve shirt (1-2)	coat
hat	warm hat	gloves
shorts (3-4)	blouses (7)	underwear (7)
socks (7)	spare shoes	raincoat
sweater	windbreaker	sweatshirt
swim suit	water shoes	

Personal

Bible	daily Bible reading guide	books
hymnal, songs	CDs	tapes
books on tape	laptop	printer
paper	adaptor	phone cord
e-mail addresses	postcard addresses	stamps
cameras x4	film	

RV	pharm &	food
itinerary	toothbrush	cocoa
maps	toothpaste	health bars
tour guides	deodorant	breakfasts
campground guides	shampoo	chicken
passport	rinse	suppers
car reg. etc.	brush	ice cream
towels	sunblock	fruit
bedding	pain spray	yogurt
sheets	itch stuff	Coke, Diet Rite
comforters	1st aid kit	Emergen-C
pillows	Tums	juice mix
seat cushion	immodium	water bottle
back rest	ibuprofen	veggies
bungies	eye drops	
phone		

pets		TO DO	
dog food	litter liners	get trav ✓s	transfer files to laptop
cat food	dog treats	get cash	
leash	flea/tick stuff	itinerary to friend	
litter box	heart worm	cancel papers	
health cert.	vet contact info	arrange for mail	

Tools for Packing
- Keep your packing list on your computer.
- Adapt it to the specific needs of each trip, then print it out.
- Check items off as you pack them.
- Make sure you easily get at things you will use often.
- Pack children's clothes within their reach.
- Buy enough baskets or containers to keep things together.
- Remember clothes for potential bad weather.
- Provide clothes for special occasions.
    - dress shoes and underwear
    - coat or jacket
- Store everything securely, so it won't slide around and get lost.
- Have bathroom and laundry supplies portable.

Four TIPS for Major Essentials
1. Make sure shower supplies are separable, portable, and clean.
    a. Color code toothbrushes and towels, or color code the baskets they're in.
    b. Each person should have their own, easily identifiable shower basket or tote.
    c. Soap should be in a soapbox; toothbrushes in a cover.
2. Install extra hooks or towels racks for drying towels, swim suits, and so forth.
3. What special food must you have: personal passions and addictions, comfort food, food for motion sickness, …
4. Pack comfort books (kids and adults alike). Reference books (concordance, flower and animal identification, …).

Tools for Figuring Out Your Vacation Style
What's your preference?
- Important objectives OR sightseeing along the way
- See everything available at each stop OR just the high points
- Keep moving OR set up camp for several days
- Detailed list of goals and activities OR general plan for the trip with flexibility OR open span of time
- LIST amenities essential for overnight stops
- LIST activities to participate in when you stop
- Are you flexible enough to change your plans if something more interesting comes along?

<u>Tools for Planning an Itinerary</u>
Ask yourself:
- Where am I going and why?
- How long can I be out, and how far can I go in a day (covered in chapter 5)?
- Have I read tour books to see what's along the way?
- Have I allowed time for extras, flat tires, laundry, and weather problems?
- Does everyone in the family have something they really want to do?

See Appendix B: Resource Materials for information on tour guidebooks.

<u>Eight TIPS for Web Sites Listing Odd or Large Things to See</u>
1. Large Canadian Roadside Attractions: Trans-Canada Highway
   http://www.roadsideattractions.ca/tch.htm
2. Roadside America: Guide to Uniquely Odd Tourist Attractions
   http://www.roadsideamerica.com/
3. World's Largest Roadside Attractions
   http://www.wlra.us/
4. World's Largest Things Traveling Roadside Attraction
   http://www.worldslargestthings.com/
5. Canada, Home to Large Roadside Attractions
   http://www.buzzle.com/editorials/7-5-2005-72661.asp
6. 59 Jaw-Dropping Roadside Attractions: Southwest
   http://budgettravelonline.com/bt-dyn/content/article/2006/06/05/AR2006060500673.html
7. Wikipedia: Roadside Attractions
   http://en.wikipedia.org/wiki/Roadside_attraction
8. 43 Places: Interesting Places in Your City
   http://www.43places.com/

<u>Tools for Planning Local Trips</u>
- Decide how far can you go after work or school on Friday.
- Mark that distance and draw a circle on your map.
- Check with the Chamber of Commerce, friends, the Internet—what's to do in that area?
- Do it!

Six TIPS for Having Fun When You're Stranded Somewhere
In bad weather, if you have car trouble, when you're hopelessly lost:
1. Go to the library.
2. Get tourist info fliers at the campground, motel/hotel office.
3. Check at the Visitor Center, Chamber of Commerce.
4. Ask at the grocery store, gas station, etc.
5. Look in the phone book.
6. Ask questions:
   What is there to do around here?
   What's this town/area known for?
   What should I see while I'm here?

Tools for Finding a Campground
- Campground guides:
   o   AAA TourBooks and Campground Guides
   o   KOA Campground Directory
   o   *Trailer Life* from the Good Sam Club
   o   SKPs
- Google "campground" and the state or nearest city
- Watch for signs along the highway

Four TIPS for Campground Activities
1. Take advantage of campground amenities
   Use the pool. Check out the game room. Are there bikes or miniature golf? An ice cream social, breakfast or dinner, movie night or special speakers?
2. Walk around, and keep your eyes open!
   Make a list of out-of-state license plates. Play an alphabet game, looking for things that start with A, then B, and so forth. Count the pets, and types of pets (I meet a caged rabbit at a KOA; my beagle was thrilled!). Notice the different things people put in their yards: statues, plants, lights. Notice the scenery, the natural plants, changes in the sky.
3. Take care of routine busy-work.
   Do the laundry. Clean and organize the RV. Wash the windows. Dump your holding tanks, and top off your fresh water.
4. Take some personal space.
   Check your email. Read a book. Watch a movie. Take a nap. Read through tourist fliers (available in the campground office). Update your trip log. Write postcards.

<u>Tools for Dealing with Feeling Lost</u>
- Don't get lost:
    - o   Plan your route.
    - o   Get directions in advance.
    - o   Mark your maps.
- Don't panic if you do get lost:
    - o   Have a compass and/or GPS system for reference.
    - o   Have a cell phone to call for help.
    - o   Don't fret or let being lost ruin your fun; calm down and know you'll come through all right.
    - o   Look for ways to enjoy yourself, wherever you wind up.

<u>Tools for Being Safe</u>
- Have a communication plan for family and friends.
- Make ID cards with emergency contact info; keep them visible in the rig.
- Hide money and credit cards in an unlikely place (under litter box, in a first aid kit).
- Sign up for an emergency protection plan for your vehicle(s).
- Use the same common sense that you use at home:
    - o   Don't be too friendly with strangers
    - o   Lock your door
    - o   Be wary, especially if you're not in a campground
    - o   Obey your internal "vibes" or concerns
- Nonetheless, have fun!

<u>Six TIPS for What to Have with You if You're Hurt and Alone</u>
1. Your health insurance card
2. Contact information for your emergency trip insurance—
    a. Care for your pets
    b. Make arrangements for children or dependents
    c. Cancel reservations later in the trip
    d. Return or store your RV
3. Phone numbers or email for your doctor, dentist, and so forth
4. Phone number or email for your lawyer
5. Phone numbers for friends who might help in an emergency
6. Phone number for your insurance agent
7. Extra credit card and debit card
8. Copies of prescriptions and spare glasses

Tools for Dealing with Those Inevitable Problems
- Know where your fuses, circuit breakers, and power switches are.
- Inform your credit card companies that you'll be traveling.
- Practice looking on the bright side.
- Ask for help when there's a problem.

Seven TIPS for Staying Safe and Happy on Drivedrivedrive Days
To keep yorself safe:
1. Stop and take a power nap if you get sleepy.
2. Take short walks to stretch your legs and restore circulation when you stop.
3. Listen to books on tape or CD.
4. Listen to and sing along with music on CD or radio; driver's choice.
5. Have snacks available within reach (in a cooler by your seat, for example), so you don't have to stop to eat.

To amuse your passengers:
1. Create a contest for who pays for mid-afternoon ice cream (most blue cars, most different license plates, most different animals spotted, ...).
2. Passengers can play board/card games (magnetic chess, checkers, etc.).
3. Play car games.
4. Passengers can do crafts (sticker books, weaving, knitting, etc.).
5. Someone can read aloud (stories, tour guides books).

Five TIPS for Safe Weather Driving
In rain, snow, sleet, ice, wind, ...
1. If it's dangerous (tornado, too-strong wind, heavy fog), get off the road:
   a. Out of your rig and into shelter
   b. Under an overpass
   c. In a rest area
   d. On the shoulder
2. Slow down (just as you would in a car).
3. Be aware: in high wind, semis and overpasses will block the wind, but then you drive back into it.
4. Stay in your lane.
5. Pray.

Ten TIPS on What You Need in Emergency Road Service (ERS)

I use Good Sam, but there are many other ERS programs out there. These are the basics to look for when you're choosing one to meet your needs:

1. 24/7 emergency dispatch service across the United States and Canada
2. Program that is focused on the needs of a large RV
3. Protection for all your family's vehicles, including bikes and boat trailers
4. Flat-tire service—repair, replace, tow
5. Locksmith if you're locked out
6. Jump starts or free tow
7. Fuel delivery if you're out of gas
8. Travel delay assistance: help with emergency travel expenses
9. Emergency medical referral service
10. Easy access to ERS personnel and information, by phone or on the Web

Tools for Traveling with a Disability

- Carry whatever aids you need:
  o Cane, wheelchair, scooter
  o Parking placard (useful to prove need)
- Know your medications:
  o Carry a copy of prescriptions
  o List medications on emergency contact card.
- Don't worry about accessibility in the US
  o Phone ahead in Canada.

Tools for Finding a Church

- Ask for church suggestions in stores, gas stations, the campground office, and fellow campers.
- Check the yellow pages, newspaper, or laundry room for lists of churches.
- Keep your eyes open as you drive into town.
- Trust the Lord to direct you.

<u>Four TIPS for Traveling with God</u>
1. Remember that He made everything and declared it was good.
   a. The heavens declare the glory of God; the skies proclaim the work of his hands (Psalm 19:1).
   b. The earth is the Lord's, and everything in it, the world, and all who live in it (Ps 24:1).
   c. Psalm 148
2. Carry a concordance or use an Internet one to find references to what you're seeing and doing: http://bible.crosswalk.com/
3. Carry a hymnal or go to an Internet hymnal; use the topical index (especially look under Nature): http://www.cyberhymnal.org/
4. Look also for references to being a stranger or traveler, journey, lost, guide, lead, beauty, creation.

<u>Tools for Wagon-Training</u>
- Be sure each person on the trip has at least one best or favorite activity to look forward to.
- Discuss variant travel styles and how to compromise.
- Have a way to communicate between vehicles.
- Have fun and unify the different groups/families (games, ice cream stops …).

<u>Tools for Sharing Your Rig</u>
- Be sure your friendship is strong enough to withstand sharing tight quarters.
- Build in ways to get some personal space.
- Give everyone some say in the itinerary and timing.
- Bring treats and surprises to brighten rain or traffic difficulties (for adults, too).
- Give your friends a packing list and chore assignments.

Tool: Chore List

____ help put awning up, down

____ help with connections (water, power, sewer)

____ help prepare and serve meals

____ help clean up after meals

____ wash dishes as necessary

____ put away dishes, meal prep materials

____ dump the trash

____ clean table, counter

____ clean floor (pick up, sweep, use vacuum)

____ shake, sweep floor mats

____ sewer dump

____ walk dog

____ feed pets

____ clean litter box

____ outside walk-around before leaving

____ inside walk-around before leaving

Tools for Keeping the Kids Happy

- Bring treats and games
- Suggest the children start a collection
- Do "junior ranger" activities in parks
- Enlist the children's suggestions for activities and stops
- Give grace; be patient—you too were young once

<u>Six TIPS for Car Games (no supplies needed, one or more players)</u>
1. Spot the alphabet
   A in underpass; b in Boston, and so forth
   Contest, one side of the road vs the other side
   Or as a group activity; or individual playing alone
   Two sources:
   - on billboards and vehicle signs
   - on license plates
2. Topical alphabet
   Name something that starts with A, then B, and so forth
   Name/explain things in alphabetical order and on a chosen topic
   - Songs (first line or title): "Amazing Grace"; "Bingo Was His Name-O"
   - Things you see along the way: ads, billboards, cat on porch
   - Things from the Bible: Adam, Babylon, cross
   - Animal names or traits: ants, birds, cawing crows
   - Things you're glad for: answered questions, babies, chewing gum
   - Whatever you can think of
3. Other alphabet games
   - I packed my grandmother's trunk, and in it I put an aardvark; I packed my grandmother's trunk, and in it I put an aardvark and a balloon; …
   - My name is Adelle; I come from Africa; I like appetizing apples. My name is Bob; I come from Burbank; I like brilliant borders.…
4. Singing games
   - Songs on a topic: animals, places, sounds, water, …
   - Songs including a certain word: big, car, …
   - Songs about things you see out the windows
5. Rhyming games
   - Spot something, name it, and give a rhyme: tree:see
   - Spot something and make a rhyming couplet: That is a tree. I wish I could ski.
   - Match lines: first player gives a first line; next player makes a rhyming line; continue until someone misses. Then start a new one: That is a car. It came from far. Twinkle twinkle little star. Jelly is in a jar. I fell down and hurt myself and it left a scar.

6. Geography

First player says a word that would be on a map, for example, Mississippi.

Next player must give a map word that starts with the last letter of the previous word: Illinois.

Singapore. Europe. East. Timbuktu. Uganda....

Words may not be repeated.

Caveat: A lot of words both begin and end with A (Australia, America ...)

Tools for Educational Opportunities

- Pick a theme
- Find connections
- Include your student
- You can learn, too

Tools for Keeping Happy Four-Footed Friends

- Have enough pet food for the trip (and buy it ahead of time, at home).
- Remember treats and chews.
- Check that the water dish is full, secure, and not going to splash.
- Bring toys, if your pet needs them.
- Carry any medication animals might need, and copies of prescriptions.
- Ask your vet about an ID chip, heartworm prevention, and flea/tick prevention.
- Bring a health certificate if you're leaving the country.
- Have a way for your vet to reach you in an emergency.

Four TIPS on the Advantages of Traveling with Your Pet

1. You're not paying for a kennel.
2. They're good company (most of the time).
3. Walking a dog (or cat!) is a great way to start a conversation.
4. They're warm in bed.

Tools for Good Neighbor Relations
- If you have bad neighbors, just deal with it—unless it's a matter of health and safety.
- Be a good neighbor:
    - o Keep kids and pets under control.
    - o Observe posted quiet hours.
    - o Be careful about loud music and shouted conversations at any hour.
    - o Clean up any spills, and use a collar to keep sewer smells down.
    - o Throw all trash away as directed.
    - o Supervise your fire, and be sure to completely extinguish it before leaving.
    - o Do unto others as you would have them do unto you.

Tools for Memory Makers
- Carry a variety of cameras:
    - o regular camera
    - o disposable backup
    - o kids' disposable
    - o panoramic
    - o waterproof
- Pack extra film.
- Store a small pocket notebook and pen in your purse, pack, or whatever you carry.
- Have a plan to store fliers, tickets, etc.
- Use a laptop or journal to keep track of what you do each day.

Eight TIPS for Simple and Useful Memory Books after the Trip
1. Take a framing or title shot: the outside of the building, the "welcome to XXX" sign, the entrance to the forest, …
2. Include people, pets, and yourself in pictures, for scale and interest.
3. Get some pictures of the entire family in special places; let the kids clown around.
4. Buy postcards for large scenery (mountains, ocean, Grand Canyon).
5. Include fliers, ads, tickets.
6. Journal daily, and add family comments about activities.
7. You can buy themed paper and stickers for the national parks, Disney Parks, and other popular attractions.
8. Create a theme for your trip: ***Fall Leaves***, ***On the Beach***, ***There and Back Again***; buy paper and stickers that match your theme.

Ten TIPS for Delightful RVing Experiences
Number 1: Have fun.
Number 2: Old and new.
Number 3: Lots to see.
Number 4: Less is more.
Number 5: Stay alive.
Number 6: Take pics.
Number 7: Think of heaven.
Number 8: Play it straight.
Number 9: Mine and thine.
Number 10: Do it again.

Appendix B:
Resource materials

AAA (American Automobile Association) TourBooks. 1-800-AAA-HELP. www.aaa.com

Compass American Guides. (Oakland, CA: Fodor's, Random House). www.fodors.com

Dummies books. (Hoboken, NJ: Wiley Publishing). Substitute state/area and most major cities for the XXX to find your title. http://www.dummies.com/WileyCDA/Section/id-100011.html

Empire State Railway Museum's Tourist Trains (Waukesha, WI: Kalmbach Publishing Co). Updated yearly; new edition comes out in February.

Frommer's. (New York, NY: Wiley). www.frommers.travelocity.com

Guidebooks from Lonely Planet (Victoria, Australia: Lonely Planet Publications).

KOA (Kampgrounds of America). http://www.koakampgrounds.com/orderadirectory/

Lonely Planet. (Victoria, Australia: Lonely Planet Publications). www.lonelyplanet.com

Milepost. Morris Communications Company, LLC. www.themilepost.com

North American Campground Directory (Ventura, CA: Woodall Publications). (877) 680-6155. http://www.woodalls.com/shop/

Off the Beaten Path. (Guilford, CT: Globe Pequot Press). www.globe-pequot.com

Trailer Life Directory. (Official Directory of the Good Sam Club). www.tldirectory.com

Traveling Literary America: A Complete Guide to Literary Landmarks. B. J. Welborn. (Lookout Mountain, TN: Jefferson Press, 2005). www.jeffersonpress.com

Appendix C:
Contact Information

AAA
American Automobile Association
1-800-AAA-HELP
www.aaa.com

AARP
American Association of Retired Persons
601 E Street NW
Washington, DC 20049
1-888-OUR-AARP (1-888-687-2277)
www.aarp.org

Airstream
www.airstream.com

Aldrich, Bess Streeter,
Bess Streeter Aldrich Foundation
PO Box 167
Elmwood, NE 68349
402-994-3855
http://www.lincolnne.com/nonprofit/bsaf/

Anton Johnson Memorial Tunnel
Whittier, AK
phone (907) 472-2327
admin@ci.whittier.ak.us
Kenai Street, BTI Suite 106
P.O. Box 608 Whittier, AK 99693
http://www.ci.whittier.ak.us/

Berlin-Ichthyosaur State Park
HC 61 Box 61200,
Austin, NV 89310
(775) 964-2440 Fax (775) 964-2012
region3@cccomm.net

Big Basin Prairie Preserve, Kansas
http://www.naturalkansas.org/bigbasin.htm

Blowing Rock, NC
http://www.blowingrock.com/
Blowing Rock Chamber of Commerce
PO Box 406—Blowing Rock, NC 28605
Visitor Center
7738 Valley Blvd. (Highway 321 Bypass)
1-800-295-7851 or 828-295-7851

Blue Ridge Parkway
199 Hemphill Knob Road
Asheville, NC 28803-8686
828 271 4779
http://www.nps.gov/blri/

Boone, IA
Boone & Scenic Valley Railroad
225 10th Street
P.O. Box 603
Boone, IA 50036
Phone: 800-626-0319
Phone: 515-432-4249
E-Mail: info@bsvrr.com

Brainerd, MN
Paul Bunyan Land is no longer in existence
http://paulbunyantrail.com/

Breckenridge, CO
http://www.townofbreckenridge.com/index.cfm
150 Ski Hill Road
PO Box 168
Breckenridge CO 80424
(970) 453-2251

Brown County State Park, IN
www.in.gov/dnr/parklake/properties/park_browncounty.html1405
State Road 46 West
Nashville, IN 47448
812-988-6406

Bryce Canyon National Park
http://www.nps.gov/brca/

Burlington carousel
http://www.burlingtoncolo.com/carousel.htm
http://www.kitcarsoncountycarousel.com/
Kit Carson County Carousel Association
P.O. Box 28
Stratton,Colorado 80836

Burr Oak, IA
Laura Ingalls Wilder Park and Museum
3603-236th Avenue,
Burr Oak, Iowa 52101
Phone 563-735-5916
www.bluffcountry.com/liwbo
The Laura Ingalls Wilder Park & Museum is located in northeast Iowa on
Highway 52, 12 miles north of Decorah and 3 miles south of Junction 52 & 44
in Minnesota.

Canby Grove Conference Center
7501 Knight's Bridge Road
PO Box 1264Canby OR, 97013
503.266.5176
http://www.canbygrove.com

Carhenge
Alliance, NE 69301
www.carhenge.com

Cat Tales Zoo, Mead WA
http://www.cattales.org/main.html
N. 17020 Newport Hwy, Mead, Washington, 99021
509. 238.4126

Cathcart, Sandy
http://sandycathcart.blogspot.com/

Celestial Seasonings
http://www.celestialseasonings.com/index_nofl.php
Celestial Seasonings Consumer Relations
The Hain Celestial Group, Inc.
4600 Sleepytime Dr.
Boulder, CO 80301
1-800-434-4246

Colorado Christian Writers Conference
http://www.writehisanswer.com/Colorado/

Colorado National Monument
Fruita, CO 81521-0001
Visitor Information
970-858-3617
http://www.nps.gov/colm/

Couer d'Alene
1621 N 3rd #100
Coeur d'Alene, ID 83816
877.782.9232
208.664.3194
http://www.coeurdalene.org/

Cypress Hills Interprovincial Park—Alberta
Box 12
Elkwater, AB
CANADA T0J 1C0
(403) 893-3777
cypress.hills@gov.ab.ca
http://www.cypresshills.com/cypresshillsab.html

Cup of Comfort
Adams Media
F+W Publications Inc.
4700 E. Galbraith Rd.
Cincinnati, OH 45236
www.adamsmedia.com

Dawson Creek
http://www.tourismdawsoncreek.com/
900 Alaska Avenue
Dawson Creek, British Columbia V1G 4T6
Telephone: (250) 782-9595
1-866-645-3022

Denali National Park
http://www.nps.gov/dena/
Denali National Park
P.O. Box 9
Denali Park, AK 99755-0009
—or—
Talkeetna Ranger Station
Box 588
Talkeetna, AK 99676
907-683-2294

Dinosaur Nat'l Monument
http://www.nps.gov/dino/
Dinosaur National Monument
4545 E. Highway 40
Dinosaur, CO 81610-9724
(970)374-3000

Dinosaur Ridge
http://www.roadsideamerica.com/attract/SDRAPdino.html
http://www.blackhillsbadlands.com/go.asp?ID=249

Dinosaur Trail, Canada
www1.travelalberta.com/content/travellingto/take.cfm?roadtripID=15

Discovery Cove, FL
http://www.discoverycove.com/explore.aspx
1-877-4-DISCOVERY

Dodge City
http://www.americanwest.com/pages/dodge.htm
Dodge City Convention & Visitors Bureau
P.O Box 1474
Dodge City, Kansas 67801
(316) 225-8186

Escapees. *See* SKPs

Estes Park Family Fun Center
http://www.what2donow.com/pages.daytrips/estesfun.html
970.586.6495
www.rideakart.com

Eugene Field House
http://www.eugenefieldhouse.org/
634 S. Broadway
St. Louis, MO 63102
314-421-4689

Exit Glacier, Kenai Fjords National Park
National Park Service
PO Box 1727
Seward, AK 99664
907-224-7500
http://www.nps.gov/kefj/index.htm

Farnell, Silvine
www.DeeperIntoPoetry.com
Silfarnell@comcast.net

Flaming Gorge Nat'l Recreation Area
http://www.utah.com/nationalsites/flaming_gorge.htm
P.O. Box 279
Manila 84046
435-784-3445

Ford, Henry. *See* Greenfield Village

Fort Clatsop National Memorial
92343 Fort Clatsop Rd
Astoria, OR 97103-9197
503-861-2471
http://www.nps.gov/focl/

Frank Slide Interpretive Centre
Box 959 Blairmore
Crowsnest Pass, Alberta T0K 0E0
Phone: (403) 562-7388
E-mail: info@frankslide.com
http://www.frankslide.com/

Four Corners, CO
http://www.utah.com/playgrounds/four_corners.htm
www.navajonationparks.org/fourcorners_monument.htm

Gambrill State Park
c/o Cunningham Falls State Park
14039 Catoctin Hollow Road
Thurmont, Md 21702
(301) 271-7574
Call 1-888-432-CAMP(2267)
www.dnr.state.md.us/publiclands/western/gambrill.html

Gateway Arch
http://www.nps.gov/jeff/index.html
11 North 4th Street
St. Louis, Missouri 63102

Gateway Arch Riverboats
http://www.gatewayarchriverboats.com/
800-878-7411

Geographic Center of the US
Lebanon, KS
http://www.roadsideamerica.com/tips/getAttraction.php3?tip_
AttractionNo==7032

Geographic Center of North America
Rugby Area Chamber of Commerce
224 Highway 2 SW
Rugby, ND 58368
Phone (701) 776-5846

Glacier National Park
http://www.nps.gov/glac/
PO Box 128
West Glacier, MT 59936
(406) 888-7800

Glenwood Springs
http://www.ci.glenwood-springs.co.us/
101 West 8th Street
Glenwood Springs, CO 81601
(970) 384-6400

Good Sam Club
1-800-234-3450
http://www.goodsamclub.com/highways/

Grand Teton National Park
http://www.nps.gov/grte/
PO Drawer 170
Moose, WY 83012-0170

Great Salt Lake
http://www.utah.com/stateparks/great_salt_lake.htm
http://www.utah.com/stateparks/antelope_island.htm
801-627-8288 or 800-255-8824
(888) 777-9771
866-867-8824

Great Smoky Mountains National Park
107 Park Headquarters Road
Gatlinburg, TN 37738
(865) 436-1200
http://www.nps.gov/grsm/

Greenfield Village
The Henry Ford
20900 Oakwood Blvd.
Dearborn, MI 48124-4088
313.982.6001
800 835 5237
http://www.hfmgv.org/

Gypsum Hills Scenic Byway
http://ksbyways.org/gyphills/
Roger Masenthin at rcandd1@ink.org
Sunflower Resource Conservation and Development
Harper, KS, or
Kaye Kuhn at ptreaty@sctelcom.net
Peace Treaty Pageant, Medicine Lodge, KS

Heber Valley Railroad
http://www.hebervalleyrr.org
450 South 600 West
Heber City, UT 84032
(435) 654-5601 SLC (801) 581-9980
reservations@hebervalleyrr.org

Indiana Dunes National Lakeshore
1100 N. Mineral Springs Road
Porter, IN 46304
219-926-7561 x225http://www.nps.gov/indu/

Jefferson National Expansion Memorial in St. Louis
http://www.nps.gov/jeff/
Jefferson National Expansion Memorial
11 N. 4th St.
St. Louis, MO 63102

Dennis Jernigan
http://www.dennisjernigan.com/
Shepherd's Heart Music
3201 N. 74th St. W.
Muskogee, OK 74401
1-800-877-0406
mail@dennisjernigan.com

Johnstown Flood Museum
http://www.nps.gov/jofl/
733 Lake Road
South Fork, PA 15956
814-495-4643
814-886-6100

Karon, Jan
http://www.mitfordbooks.com/index.asp

Kenai Fjords National Park
www.nps.gov/kefj/home.htm

Klootchy Creek OR spruce
http://lewisandclarktrail.com/section4/orcities/seaside/sitkaspruce.htm

KOA
www.KOAkampgrounds.com

Lady Washington
http://ladywashington.org/
(800) 200 LADY
GHHSA
P.O. Box 2019
Aberdeen, WA, 98520

Lagoon Amusement Park
http://www.lagoonpark.com/
Lagoon
P.O. Box 696
Farmington, Utah 84025
info@lagoonpark.com
(800) 748-5246

Lassen Volcanic National Park
P.O. Box 100
Mineral, CA 96063-0100
(530) 595-4444
http://www.nps.gov/lavo/

Land Between the Lakes
100 Van Morgan Drive
Golden Pond, KY 42211
(270) 924-2000
http://www.lbl.org/Home.html

Lewis and Clark
http://www.nationalgeographic.com/lewisandclark/

Liberty Bell
Independence National Historical Park
143 South Third Street
Philadelphia, PA 19106
http://www.nps.gov/inde/home.htm

Little Brown Church in the Vale
2730 Cheyenne Ave
Nashua, IA 50658
641-435-2027
www.littlebrownchurch.org
The church is on Highway 346, north of Waterloo, IA.

Mandan, ND
1600 Burnt Boat Drive, Bismarck, ND 58503
1-800-767-3555 or 701-222-4308
http://www.bismarckmandancvb.com/

Mansfield, MO
Laura Ingalls Wilder Historic Home and Museum
3068 Highway A
Mansfield, MO 65704
(877) 924-7126
info@lauraingallswilderhome.com
http://www.lauraingallswilderhome.com/

Mapleton IA
http://www.mapleton.com/

Mary Carey's McKinley View Lodge
www.mckinleyviewlodge.com/jean.html

Mesa Verde National Park
http://www.nps.gov/meve/
PO Box 8
Mesa Verde, CO 81330-0008
970-529-4465
970-529-4465

Milepost
1998-2005 The MILEPOST and Morris Communications Company, LLC
http://www.themilepost.com/

Moab
http://www.moabchamber.com/
217 E Center Street,
Suite #250
Moab, Utah 84532
435-259-7814
info1@moabchamber.com

Montgomery, Lucy Maud
Island Information Service
P.O. Box 2000
Charlottetown, PE
Canada
C1A 7N8
Phone: (902)368-4000
E-mail: Island@gov.pe.ca
1-888-PEI-PLAY
http://www.gov.pe.ca/lmm/index.php3

Moody, Ralph
http://www.littletongov.org/history/biographies/moody.asp

Mount Vernon, Iowa
213 First Street West
Mount Vernon, IA 52314
(319) 895-8742
cmv@cityofmtvernon.com
http://www.cityofmtvernon.com/

National Statesman
earldodge@dodgeoffice.net

Native Heritage Center, Alaska
http://www.alaskanative.net/
8800 Heritage Center Drive
Anchorage, Alaska 99506
(907) 330-8000-

Nevada Northern RR Museum
http://nevadanorthernrailway.net/
1-866-40STEAM or 1-866-407-8326
e-mail: nnry@mwpower.net

Nevada Wide Open
Nevada Commission on Tourism
401 North Carson Street
Carson City, NV 89701
1-800-NEVADA-8
www.travelnevada.com/activities_story.asp

Niagara Falls
http://www.niagarafallsstatepark.com/
(716) 278-1796.
http://www.tourismniagara.com/

Oregon Christian Writers
http://www.oregonchristianwriters.org/

Oregon Trail Ruts
http://wyoparks.state.wy.us/ORslide.htm
Guernsey State Park
Box 429
Guernsey, WY 82214
sphs@state.wy.us

Ozarks
http://www.missouriozarks.org/
Ozark Heritage
Tourism Association
1301 Kingshighway
Rolla, Missouri 65401
1-888-809-3817
ohta@missouriozarks.org

Petrified Forest National Park
http://www.nps.gov/pefo/
P.O. Box 2217
Petrified Forest, AZ 86028
—or—
1 Park Road
Petrified Forest, 86028

Porter, Gene Stratton
limberlost@adamswells.com
Limberlost State Historic Site
PO BOX 356
GENEVA IN 46740
260-368-7428
http://www.genestrattonporter.net/

Porter, Gene Stratton
650 W. Washington Street
Indianapolis, IN 46204
317.232.1637
http://www.in.gov/ism/HistoricSites/GeneStrattonPorter/historic.asp

Prince Edward Island
Island Information Service
P.O. Box 2000
Charlottetown, PE
Canada C1A 7N8
1-888-PEI-PLAY

Prince William Sound Cruises and Tours
1-800-992-1297
513 W. 4th Ave
Anchorage
www.princewilliamsound.com

Resurrection Bay, AK
http://www.kenaifjords.com/
877-258-6877
info@ahtours.com
Alaska Heritage Tours
2525 C Street, Suite 405
Anchorage, AK 99503

Rocky Mountain National Park
http://www.nps.gov/romo/
1000 Highway 36
Estes Park, CO 80517-8397
970-586-1206

RVing Women
P.O. Box 1940
Apache Junction, AZ
85217-1940
www.rvingwomen.org

Saint Louis Zoo
One Government Drive
St. Louis, MO 63110
(800) 966-8877
http://www.stlzoo.org/contact/

Salt Lake City, UT
http://www.visitsaltlake.com/
Salt Palace Convention Center
90 South West Temple
Salt Lake City, UT 84101
801-521-2822
800-541-4955

Scott, Dred
http://www.nps.gov/jeff/dred_scott.html

SKPs
Escapees, Inc.
100 Rainbow Drive
Livingston, TX 77351
Phone 888-757-2582
Fax 936-327-4388
http://www.escapees.com/

Southern Museum of Civil War and Locomotive History
2829 Cherokee Street
Kennesaw, GA 30144
Ph. (770) 427-2117
http://www.southernmuseum.org/contact.html

Storyeum
142 Water Street
Gastown
Vancouver, BC
Canada V6B 1B2
http://www.storyeum.com
Ph: 604.687.8142
TF: 800.687.8142

Sumpter Valley Narrow Gauge RR
http://www.svry.com/
roger@railroadsusa.com
Sumpter Valley Railroad
P.O. Box 389, Baker City, OR 97814-0389
(541) 894-2268 or Toll Free (866) 894-2268 (June-September)
(541) 523-3453 Winter Months (October-May)
svrydepotstaff@eoni.com

Swift, Jonathan
Swift's map of Brobdingnag: www.jaffebros.com/lee/gulliver/bancroft/6.jpeg

Tok, AK
info@tokalaska.com
http://www.tokalaska.com/

Trail Ridge Road, CO
http://www.nps.gov/romo/visit/weather/scenicdrives.html

Trailer Life Directory
www.tldirectory.com

Twain, Mark
http://www.hanmo.com/
(866)263-4825

Wallen, Jan
http://www.sellingyourexpertise.com/jan.htm

Washington, D.C. tourism
http://www.dcregistry.com/sights.html

Watson Lake, Yukon
P.O. Box 590
Watson Lake, Yukon, Canada Y0A 1C0
Tel: 867-536-7778
Fax: 867-536-7522
E-mail: twl@northwestel.net
http://www.yukoninfo.com/watson/signpostforest.htm

Webster Groves, MO
http://www.webstergroves.org/
314-963-5300 #4 E. Lockwood
Webster Groves, MO 63119

Whitewater Valley Railroad
P.O. Box 406
Connersville, IN 47331
(765) 825-2054
http://www.whitewatervalleyrr.org/excursions/

Wilder, Laura Ingalls
Laura Ingalls Wilder Historic Home and Museum
3068 Highway A
Mansfield, MO 65704
(877) 924-7126
info@lauraingallswilderhome.com
http://www.lauraingallswilderhome.com/
other Laura Ingalls Wilder sites:
http://www.littlehousebooks.com/index.html
http://www.lauraingallswilder.com/

Wolf Park
Battle Ground, IN
wolfpark@wolfpark.org
www.wolfpark.org

Yellowstone National Park
P.O. Box 168
Yellowstone National Park, WY 82190-0168
307-344-7381
http://www.nps.gov/yell/home.htm

Yellowstone Bear World
http://www.yellowstonebearworld.com/
6010 South 4300 West Rexburg, ID
5 Miles South
of Rexburg on
U.S. Highway 20
Phone: 208.359.9688

Yosemite National Park
http://www.nps.gov/yose/
Superintendent
P.O. Box 577
Yosemite National Park, CA 95389
209-372-0200

Zion National Park
SR 9
Springdale, UT 84767-1099
(435) 772-3256
http://www.nps.gov/zion/

Appendix D: Glossary

5th-wheel—a towed RV that is hitched in the body of a pickup truck
AC—air conditioning
adaptors—different plug ends so you can connect any cord to any receptacle
ADA—Americans with Disabilities Act
airport—wireless Internet access for a Macintosh computer
antifreeze, RV—RVs use non-poisonous antifreeze, since it goes in the water pipes.
basement—outside storage areas
bay—outside storage area
black water—water and so forth from the toilet
boondocking—camping without electrical or other hookups
cab-over bed—the bed over the driver's seat area in a Class C RV
cable—any electrical cord
caravan—a group of RVs traveling together
city water—water from the faucet in the campground rather than your tanks
Class A—an RV that looks like a bus, with a flat vertical front; they ride high on the road
Class C—an RV that looks like a pickup truck, with an extension over the driver's area
collar (dump)—a rubber or plastic connector that gives a relatively tight fit between the dump hose and the sewer in the ground
connections—any wire or hose from the RV to the campground: electric, water, cable, etc.
cruise control—allows you to set the engine to keep you at a desired speed
dial-up—connecting to the Internet with a phone cord
drivedrivedrive—my family's term for days with no tourist stops, just cranking out the mileage
dry camping—camping without electrical or other hookups
dump—empty the contents of holding tanks into a tank in the ground
emergency road service—insurance-type coverage for flat tires, being out of gas, or having other problems with your rig on the road
ERS—Emergency Road Service
family radio—a type of walkie-talkie
fifth-wheel—see 5th-wheel

fish-eye lens—a lens that focuses your view so you can see directly behind and below you

gates (to dump)—the opening to the black and gray holding tanks

generator—runs on gasoline and provides regular electricity; allows you to run your AC or microwave without being connected to shore power

GFI—Ground Fault Interrupter: a safety device that turns off the power in case of water or other interference with the electricity

GPS—Global Positioning System: an electronic gizmo that talks with satellites and tells you precisely where you are

gray water—water from the sinks and shower

historical marker—a sign on the side of the road telling you about significant events

holding tanks—the tanks that hold your black and gray water

hookups—connections

id chip—a tiny computer chip injected under the skin of an animal; it can be scanned (similar to grocery store scanners) and give vets contact information for a lost pet

inverter—turns battery power into regular electricity

itinerary—written plan of where you're going and when

journal—written log of what you've done, thought, and seen each day

leveling blocks—blocks of plastic or wood that you can use to raise one wheel of your rig when parked on a slope

license plate game—when you see a license plate, check off the state or province from your list; the goal is to find all of them (good luck!)

mileage—how many miles per gallon you get on the road; also used for distance between two points

modem—way of connecting to the Internet

MOM switch—provides momentary or auxiliary power when your battery is low

navigator—sits in the passenger seat and reads the itinerary, tracks you on the map, watches for highway exits, and so forth

navigator's seat—passenger seat

odometer—keeps track of how many miles you have driven

pickup camper—a pickup truck with a little camper shell/cover in the bed

pop-up—a trailer with canvas sides; roof cranks up and beds pull out

pressure regulator—screws onto your water hose and keeps the water pressure within safe limits

pull-through site—site in a campground open at both ends; you pull in from one end and pull out the other in the morning (so, no backing!)

rally (club)—a group of RVers camping together, often taking classes or doing activities together

rear-monitor camera—shows what is behind your rig on a view screen by the driver's seat

register—sign in at a campground, just like at a motel

reservations—phone ahead and make sure the campground has a place for your rig—RV, trailer, etc.

self-contained—everything you need (bathroom, kitchen, etc.) is in your rig

shore cable—the power cord that plugs into an outlet at the campground

shore power—electricity from a source other than your rig

slide/slide-out—part of the living area that slides out when you're camped, providing extra space

spot mirrors—the little mirrors below or in your regular rear-view mirrors (the "object in mirror is closer than it appears" mirror)

storage bay/bin—storage area behind doors around the bottom and outside of your RV

"summerize"—my joke on winterize; it means to get the rig ready to go on the road after it's been stored all winter

tour books—books telling you interesting things to see and do in a particular area

tourist trap—an overpriced, over-advertised tourist stop with little value for your money

tow/toad—tow is to pull a trailer or car; toad is a joke on towed-vehicle and refers to the car you are towing

trip log—a journal or record of what you've done each day

wagon-train—two or more RVs traveling together

walk-around—walk all the way around the rig; a safety activity to make sure it's safe to pull out of your campsite

WiFi—wireless Internet access

winterize—prepare the RV for storage over the winter

Index

To contact Elsi Dodge, find out more about the travels of the Meandering Moose, or share your adventures or questions, please go to:

www.RVTourist.com

or email:

ElsiDodge@RVTourist.com

About the Author

Elsi Dodge is a single woman who has been traveling in a recreational vehicle much of her life. Her trips range from weekend jaunts to one to two months. In addition, she vacations with friends, in her RV as well as wagon-train style. She has owned both Class C and Class A self-contained vehicles. She researches and plans her trips so that she will see and do as much as possible but gladly changes her itinerary when something better comes along. In her RV, Dodge, with her dog and cat, enjoys all the comforts of home as she drives through the wilds of America.

When she's not traveling, Dodge lives in Boulder, Colorado. Lady, her elderly beagle, loves playing in the fenced yard or lying in the sun, waiting for someone to come pat her. Dolphin stalks dinosaurs from window to window (and doesn't understand why they are called squirrels and blue jays). His innocent tabby-cat demeanor comes undone when he spots an open-toed shoe, and he changes to a saber-toothed tiger and attacks.

Dodge reads widely and frequently, sings in her church choir, and works with the youth group at the Boulder Chinese Baptist Church. Although she is retired from teaching special needs children in the public schools, she volunteers at a small Christian school, tutors, mentors Chinese women needing help with their English in college-level classes, and serves as an advocate for families needing guidance through the school system.

She has completed the Apprentice and Journeyman courses of the Christian Writers Guild. She loves to attend writing conferences such as the Oregon Christian Writers Summer Conference in August near Portland, Oregon, and Colorado Christian Writers each May in Estes Park, Colorado. Dodge is a member of Boulder Christian Writers, a critique group.

Her devotionals, poetry, stories, and articles have been published in:

- *Highways*, Official Publication of the Good Sam Club (November 2006)
- *His Forever* (www.adamsmedia.com)
- *Today's Christian* (www.christianitytoday.org)
- Nevada Wide Open (http://www.travelnevada.com/activities_story.asp)
- Oregon Christian Writers newsletter (http://www.oregonchristianwriters.org/columns/fall06/spotlight.htm)
- *Cup of Comfort Devotional Guide for Women* (www.addamsmedia.com)
- "Live," Radiant Life (www.gospelpublishing.com)
- "Harvest" from Mission to the Americas (www.mta.org)
- Fire by Nite, spring 2005 contest winner
- KOA (Kampgrounds of America) Web site (www.koakampgrounds.com)
- *RVing Women* (www.rvingwomen.org)
- *Quiet Hour* (www.cookministries.com)
- *National Statesman* (earldodge@dodgeoffice.net)
- *Bethany Church Lenten Guide* (www.bethanyboulder.org)

→ Side Trip to WaKeeney, Kansas
September, 2003

The tinge of red to the east is highlighted with pinks and oranges. Soon the clouds on the eastern horizon seem to be drenched in molten lava. A bird erupts into song. Others add harmony and counterpoint. The air is filled with color and music.

I stand enthralled while the dog sniffs around the bushes. The sky's color is reflected across the wheat fields.

The sun moves higher, the colors pale, until I am facing a blue sky with bits of gray cloud.

As I'm disconnecting the power and water, I wonder, *why am I thinking about Christmas?*

Finally it dawns on me. And I leave the campground, singing, "*And heaven and nature sing! And heaven and nature sing! And heaven, and heaven and nature sing!*" ("Joy to the World," Isaac Watts)

To contact Elsi Dodge, find out more about the travels of the Meandering Moose, or share your adventures or questions, please go to:

www.RVTourist.com

or email:

ElsiDodge@RVTourist.com

978-0-595-41532-8
0-595-41532-6

Printed in the United States
73113LV00005BA/127-309